You, the Sentencer
- What Would You Choose?

by John Ebrington

Introduction

Welcome to "You the Sentencer - What Would You Choose?"

The Aim of this Book:
The aim of this book is to give people an insight into the realities of crime and to the process of sentencing people at Court. There is possibly a tendency to instantly consider all offenders as criminals that deserve to be punished. However, in this book you will access the human side of crime, based upon real crimes, real victims and real people who commit offences.

Hopefully, you will get a real insight into offences that take place, the real backgrounds of offenders and the possible reasons why the offences took place. You will also get an insight into the role of the Probation Service and possible strategies designed to help people stop offending.

Through reading this book, I very much hope that you will also be encouraged to consider steps that we, as a society, could take to reduce crime. People seem to thirst for tougher prison sentences to be dispensed as a deterrent to crime, but I would argue that this strategy hasn't worked. I would much rather encourage people to think of ways of reducing numbers of our nation's children growing up into criminals. In other words, encourage people to identify the root causes of crime and consider ways of tackling these. People from all walks of life commit crimes and by following people's life stories in this book will perhaps explain why they have done so.

Finally, I would like you to consider what would you do when faced with various difficult situations that could possibly bring you close to breaking the law. Many people will be unaware of some of the rights and wrongs that we discuss in this book, which leads me to suggest that they should perhaps be taught in schools. However, there are not rights and wrongs for all of the dilemmas in the final section of the book. The aim of these other dilemmas, as is the general aim of this book, is to encourage people to become more understanding, kinder and more considerate towards each other.

What this book contains and what we shall asking you to do:

Court Interview Role Plays
I shall first of all be asking you to read through some extracts of fictional Court Report interviews. These will give you a small insight into the interview process.

I shall in particular be asking you to carefully assess the offenders' answers. On occasion, their version of events may differ from that of the victim and these need to be spotted and noted, as well as the offenders' attitudes towards the victim, towards their own offences and previous offending. For example, I shall be asking you to consider whether the offender is expressing any appropriate remorse for their actions based on their answers and what you might consider is the risk of them reoffending.

Realistic Court Reports
This book contains a series of realistic fictional Court reports based upon real, actual events, which I would ask you to read and then decide what sentence you would impose on the offender in each case. After each report is a questionnaire and commentary section.

Difficult Scenarios. What would you choose to do?
In this final section I place you in various difficult theoretical situations and ask you what would you choose to do in these different circumstances. These will hopefully be entertaining and thought provoking. You may even find that some of these may even possibly bring you close to breaking the law. The slightly humbling point being, that it may be easier to break the law than you think. Many people will be unaware of some of the rights and wrongs discussed in this book and it seems a shame that they are not to be found on the school syllabuses. However, there will not be definite rights and wrongs to all of the scenarios. The aim here is

to encourage people to become more solution focussed, kinder and more supportive towards each other.

What steps could be taken to block people's pathways into crimes?
Aside from making examples of people in Court, I shall also be asking you to think about what sort of constructive steps could society take to reduce similar offences occurring in future. What sort of things in their lives could have stopped the people, who became offenders, from offending in the first place? What steps could be taken by society to block people's pathways into crime?

Ideas will hopefully come to you when you read about people's backgrounds. For example, I recall one case where the young man who began to commit thefts in order to fund his drug addiction. He had a fairly normal upbringing except that his father and his grandfather were not particularly positive role models as they openly used to smoke cannabis in front of him. The young man had a stutter and was particularly shy around girls at school. He was first introduced to cocaine by his friends' parents who gave it him on a night out as a way of overcoming his shyness with young women.

He became addicted to drugs and began to commit thefts to fund his habit. What steps could have been taken that would have helped him not to have become a criminal?

Many offenders have been victims themselves
You will see from some reports that a number of offenders have previously been victims themselves. All victims deserve every support after an offence has been committed against them.

One aspect of the successful "Anti-knife crime" project in Glasgow is that professionals spend some time with the victims of knife crime. Assistance is given to the victims to help them get their lives 'back on track' in a positive direction so as to avoid becoming a victim again. The victims are in particular discouraged from carrying knives for protection too.

Who am I?
I am a retired Probation Officer who has written this book under the pseudonym of John Ebrington. I first joined the Probation Service in my mid-thirties, having previously been in the Hotel and Catering Industry. I initially worked in Probation in a voluntary capacity and then worked part time supervising Community-Service Projects in the community. I was encouraged to apply for the role as a Community Service Officer and was successful. I greatly enjoyed the job and after several years my line manager encouraged me to train to become a Probation Officer. I then completed a University Course aged in my mid-thirties. When I first qualified, I initially worked as a Probation Officer in a busy part of London.

Although very stressful at times, I greatly enjoyed the

job. In doing it, I felt that I had at last found the right niche for me in life. Basically, I feel that I am a people person, that likes working with people in a positive way. As I was growing up my parents faced remarkable challenges in life that were both humbling and a learning curve for me. I have learnt to be quite philosophical at times and I always tend to believe that in most situations, out of bad, can come good.

What are the origins of the Court reports?
The reports are based upon notes prepared for actual reports that were mostly written in the 1990's that have all now been anonymised. All of the people's names and the place names have been changed. Details about the offences and people's background details have also been changed. All of the offences took place sometime ago and all of those originally involved have now moved on and are now unlikely to be able to recognise themselves.

What are the reports based upon?
The Probation Officer preparing the report will normally receive a copy of the prosecution papers. These will include a summary of the facts of the case, witness statements and a record of previous convictions. The officer will study these and make an assessment about the seriousness of the offence and the offender's attitude to it. The officer will consider what caused the offence and make an assessment of the risk to the public from further possible offending. In doing this, the officer will look for any patterns in previous offending behaviour.

Most importantly, the Prosecution papers will contain statements from the victims of the offence. The Probation Officer will take the views and experiences of the victims into account, whilst interviewing the defendant and in preparing the report. The Probation Officer will make careful note of any attempts by the offender to minimise their offence, or to put forward a different account of the events than that of the victim. The defendant's attitude towards the victim is also important too. Should the defendant be made subject to a Probation Order, the experiences of the victim will be used in trying to get the offender to empathise and fully understand the views and feelings of the victim.

For the Court interview the Probation Officer will interview the defendant for about an hour or so and the report is largely based upon the outcomes of this interview. Quite a lot of skill is involved in conducting these interviews.

What skills do you think are needed to conduct these Court Report interviews?

It is crucial for the offender to fully understand why they are there. The role of the Probation Service is to be independent of the prosecution and the defence and to offer an impartial assessment of the offender and their offending to those sentencing and to look for ways of reducing any likelihood of reoffending.

It is important to put the offender at ease and to enable them to speak freely.

After each Court Report is a commentary section which will have my own observations and learning points from the report.

In contrast to all of the formality of the Court Reports, these sections are more relaxed and informal. There will be some interesting anecdotal stories about my experiences and discussion points.

In this section I shall be asking you how you would sentence the offender you have just read about, steps that could have possibly been taken in the person's life to divert them from committing crimes and about what steps could be taken by society in general to reduce such crimes from happening in future.

I shall be asking you all sorts of other questions to answer too. For example, why is it that in the UK, women commit considerably less offences than men? What do you think would have happened to the offender if they were sentenced to a term of imprisonment?

Sentencing people to longer terms of imprisonment has not worked
Many people believe that the way to deal with crime in the UK is to become more punitive, bring in tougher sentences and sentence more people to imprisonment and impose longer prison sentences. There is a common notion that we have as a society become softer upon crime and that prisons have become far too comfortable. Well, I can assure you the reverse is true. Offenders

are now being sentenced to considerably longer Prison Sentences for certain crimes than they were 50 years ago and current conditions in UK prisons are now significantly worse than they were 50 years ago. Our current prisons are hopelessly over- crowded and understaffed. Violence, drug abuse, self-harm and suicides have gone up significantly, leading to many offenders' behaviour becoming much more problematic having been in prison, than before they went in. Offenders are today leading less productive lives in Prisons than they were 50 years ago. Less time is spent educating prisoners and rehabilitating them.

Offenders released from prison without somewhere to live are much more likely to reoffend. Offenders released from prison with worse drug problems than when they went in, are also more likely to reoffend. Stable accommodation, settled relationships and regular employment are all factors that help people avoid reoffending.

Changes to Community Sentences supervised by the Probation Service over the years.
There have been constant changes. The concept of Community Service came up in the 1970's. The idea of it is for offenders to repay society for their crimes by undertaking a number of hours work for the benefit of the local community. This could involve helping redecorate a local village hall, helping OAPs with their gardens or working for a local charity. The work is supposed to be either physically or emotionally

demanding. It should not replace somebodies' regular paid employment but rather undertake much needed work that otherwise would not have been done.

Over the years, Community Service has been continuously renamed and repackaged as something new and tougher called "Community Pay-back" and "Unpaid Work", whilst remaining essentially exactly the same Community Service, but with a few new brass knobs on, such as the wearing of bright fluorescent jackets.

Probation Orders have now been replaced. An overarching Community Sentence can now be imposed that is supervised by the Probation Service. A number of different requirements can now be added to the Community Sentence, such as a Curfew Order and/or requirement to attend Probation Supervision, or attendance to different offending behaviour groups designed to address various issues such Anger Management and Drug and Alcohol Problems.

Whilst this has had a beneficial impact in being able to provide a range of Community Sentences designed to address offending behaviours there has been tendency to sentence people to more things for lesser offences. Therefore in 1980, a person would have been sentenced to a 100 hours Community Service for a particular offence as a strict alternative to custody. If they failed to comply, they would be sentenced to imprisonment. Today for the same offence they would probably be sentenced to 24 months- probation supervision, a requirement to attend an offending behaviour group, a curfew order and 180 hours Unpaid work, but not always as a strict alternative to custody.

The sentencing framework for community orders is set out in the Criminal Act 2003 ("the 2003 Act"). The 2003 Act created a single community order which allows courts to tailor community orders to fit the crimes of individual offenders by providing courts with the ability to create a community order containing one or more requirements drawn from a menu of at least twelve. A community order can contain any number of the following requirements:

- Unpaid work (known as community service or community payback);

- Residence (requiring an offender to reside at a place specified in the court order);

- Mental health treatment;

- Drug rehabilitation;

- Alcohol treatment;

- Supervision (requiring an offender to attend appointments with probation officer);

- Attendance centre (requiring offenders under 25 to

attend a particular centre at specified times);

- Prohibited activity (requiring an offender to refrain from participating in certain activities as set out in the court order);

- Curfew (confining an offender to his or her home for a specified number of hours per day);

- Exclusion (prohibiting the offender from entering a place specified in the court order);

- Programme (requiring the offender to participate in an accredited programme such as anger management courses);

- Activity (requiring the offender to participate in certain activities such as attend basic skills classes).

Courts are also able to impose a foreign travel prohibition requirement and an alcohol abstinence and monitoring requirement.

INTRODUCTION

YOU, THE SENTENCER - WHAT WOULD YOU CHOOSE?

Contents

MOCK INTERVIEWS

Before sharing the Court Reports with you, I would like you to complete two mock interviews. This will involve you reading the facts of the case and then making an assessment of the defendants' answers to various questions. This will involve you assessing their attitudes, truthfulness, good and bad points and level of remorse for their offending. I shall be asking you to make comments about the defendants' answers and identifying any concerns you may have and further questions you would like to ask the defendant.

Section 1 27
Court Report Interview 1

Section 2 35
Court Report Interview 2

AIMS OF THE COURT INTERVIEW AND POSSIBLE TECHNIQUES.

In this section some of the practical aims and techniques I used to deploy in interviewing people are discussed

Section 3 45
Interview Techniques and Aims of the Court Report Interview

COURT REPORTS SECTION

Section 4 49
A Violent Offence Committed by a Young Woman
Report 1

Section 5 59
Attitudes Towards Women and Crime
Commentary on Court Report 1

Section 6 69
A Violent Offence Against the Police
Report 2

Section 7 79
Assault Police
Case Commentary on Court Report 2

Section 8 83
A Victim of Crime Commits an Offence
Report 3

Section 9 95
Life Experiences can Undoubtably Contribute to Becoming an Offender
Case Commentary on Court Report 3

Section 10 99
The Case of a Persistent Sex Offender
Report 4

Section 11 115
Trying to Protect the Public from Sex Offenders
Case Commentary on Court Report 4

Section 12 125
Many Offenders Start Offending as Children
Report 5

Section 13 137
The Younger People Start Offending, the More Persistent They Become
Commentary on Court Report 5

Section 14 143
Complete Denial of Any Responsibility for Serious Offences
Report 6

Section 15 157
Teamwork is Key in Working with Offenders
Commentary on Court Report 6

Section 16 163
A Mentally Unwell Person Gets Caught Up in the Criminal Justice System
Report 7

Section 17 173
Mentally Ill People Need to be Better Cared for
Commentary on Court Report 7

Section 18. 177
   Acute Attention Seeking Behaviour
   Report 8

Section 19. 189
   All of the Agencies Turned Their Backs on Him
   Commentary on Report 8

Section 20. 199
   A Post Office Prosecution that Revealed Post Office
   Incompetence
   Report 9

Section 21. 207
   Not Only Were the Post Office Incompetent, so Were the Police
   Commentary Court Report 9

Section 22. 213
   An Unusual Offence of Indecent Behaviour by a Woman
   Report 10

Section 23. 223
   When a Probation Officer Witnesses Someone they are
   Supervising Commit an Offence
   Commentary on Court Report 10

Section 24. 233
   Suitability for Parole Report
   Report 11

Section 25 245
   Police Corruption and Crimes Committed by Police Officers
   Commentary on Parole Report

Section 26 257
   Route Map for Tackling Offending
   Report 12

Section 27 271
   A Problematic Childhood Can Lead to Becoming an Offender
   Commentary Court Report 12

Section 28 277
   Low Depths of Drug Addictions
   Report 13

Section 29 289
   Lack of Resources to Help People With Addictions in the 1990's
   Commentary Court Report 13

Section 30 295
   A Professional Criminal Has Enough of Committing Crimes and Cooperates with the Police
   Report 14

Section 31 307
   A New Scheme Designed to Tackle Persistent Offenders
   Commentary Report 14

Section 32. 317
   How People's Lives Can Change for the Better
   Court Report 15

Section 33. 327
   Assault at the Probation Office
   Commentary on Report 15

Section 34. 331
   A Man Obsessed About Cars
   Court Report 16

Section 35. 335
   At Last, a Positive Outcome
   Commentary on Report 16(Deferred Sentence)

Section 36. 339
   Upper-Class Man Commits an Offence
   Court Report 17

Section 37. 353
   Concern Must Be Expressed About Our Politicians
   Commentary on Court Report 17

WHAT WOULD YOU DO?

In this section, I pose you lots of different difficult dilemmas that I hope you will find entertaining, stimulating and thought provoking. You will be asked what, would you, do in these various situations. Some of them may even bring you close to possibly theoretically breaking the law. Many questions will also be encouraging people to hopefully adopt a more considerate approach towards each other too. You will also be asked what things could be done to reduce crime in the UK.

In section 39 are some difficult dilemmas that are best usefully debated amongst a group of people if possible. By doing this, I am hoping to encourage people to adopt a more considerate approach towards each other in society.

Section 38 365
What Would You Choose?

Section 39 375
Difficult Dilemmas

YOU, THE SENTENCER - WHAT WOULD YOU CHOOSE?

Section 1

Court Report Interview 1

Instructions:
You are at the Probation Office and you are about to interview someone for the Court Report you are going to write about them.

You first need to read through the facts of the case and make an assessment of the seriousness of the offence. During the interview you will give the defendant an opportunity to give their version of the offence and give an explanation for their actions.

You will need to make an assessment of the defendant's truthfulness and willingness to take responsibility for their actions and their level of remorse for what they have done.

You will be making note of their attitudes, their background and any good and bad points about them.

You are asked to make note of any observations or concerns you might have about their answers.

You will need to consider what follow up questions you would like to ask the defendant.

Facts of the case.
The Police observed a car being driven very slowly and falteringly along the Cardiff Road at an estimated speed of 10 – 15 mph. It was at around 5pm on a busy dark, November, Tuesday evening. The Police initially thought that there might be a mechanical problem with the vehicle and as it was causing a potential hazard, they flagged down the car to see if the driver needed assistance.

However, upon speaking with the driver, Susan Hampshire, it became immediately apparent that she had been drinking.

Her 8-year-old disabled daughter was a passenger in the car. A roadside breathalyser breath test was administered. Ms Hampshire was found to be about twice over the limit with a reading of 70 mg in her breath.

Upon being arrested, Susan Hampshire stated, "Oh dear, my husband is going to be very cross with me, as his dinner won't be on the table when he gets home."

She was taken to the police station where she was given a blood test. She was found to have 160 ml of alcohol in her blood, which is about twice the legal limit.

In Ms Hampshire's handbag was found a pack of Benzodiazepines, which had a label on the packet confirming they had been prescribed to her.

On being charged Ms Hampshire stated, "I am sorry to be such a nuisance to you and to every-body".

Ms Hampshire was convicted of driving with excess alcohol two years ago, when she was issued with a £300 fine and banned from driving for 12 months.

> **Having read the above facts of this case what concerns do you have? What follow up questions would you like to ask her?**

The defendant, Susan Hampshire's version of the offence:

"I am so sorry about what happened. I do tend to worry and get anxious over things. My husband works as a Senior Fire Brigade Officer and normally gets home at 6.30pm and expects his cooked dinner to be on the table when he comes in. Every Tuesday night he likes to eat Grilled Gammon steak, garnished with pineapple, chips, peas and a fried egg. I got anxious that I'd forgotten to buy his gammon steak, when I did the weekend shop. I thought that I had better nip out and buy the Gammon steak before he came home. I knew that I had been drinking, but didn't think I'd had too much and I didn't want to face my husband's anger if he didn't have his dinner ready when he came in.

I took my daughter Nina with me, because I couldn't leave her on her own at home. She has a learning disability. My mother used to help with her care, but my Mum passed away two years ago. That Tuesday, was the anniversary of her passing. I was upset and I think that I drank about 6 or 8 glasses of wine on that day.

I normally don't drink more than a bottle of wine per week because my husband Ronald doesn't like it.

I was prescribed the Benzodiazepines medication to treat my Anxiety. I know that you are advised not to drink alcohol when taking Benzodiazepines. I am really sorry about what I did, as I now appreciate that I put people at risk on the roads through what I did."

> **What concerns might you have about what Susan Hampshire has said and what follow up questions would you ask her?**

How did you get on at school Susan?

Susan Hampshire tells us about her school days:

"It was okay really. My favourite subjects were chemistry and domestic science. I was quite good at maths too, but kept quiet about it in class.

I gave up chemistry because it was more of a subject

for boys really. The careers adviser suggested, I should do hairdressing at college, but I wasn't sure really, as I had no interest in doing it. There didn't seem many other options for women other than hairdressing or low paid packing boxes work in a factory which was done by women. I left school without any qualifications."

Has Susan's reply raised any concerns and would you ask her any follow up questions?

Tell us about your employment history Susan?

Susan tells us about her employment history:

"I see my main job as being a housewife really. I take pride in looking after my home and like to do a good job of it. My husband tells me he likes it all spick and span looking and to lower my standards for no-one.

I do a part-time job as a cleaner and give all of my wages to my husband. It's only fair as he pays all of the bills.

The rest of the time I look after our daughter. She is 8 years old and has a learning disability. She needs quite of a lot of care and looking after. It gets me down a bit sometimes as there is such a lot to do."

Does Susan's response give you cause for concern? Would you ask any follow up questions?

Tell us about your health issues Susan and why you have been prescribed Benzodiazepines?

Susan tells us about her health issues:

> *"I have always had anxiety issues ever since I was a child. I was lacking in self-confidence and never said boo to a goose. I used to just sit there in class and never used to say any-thing. I was so nervous that I used to get picked on by the other children and that just made my anxiety worse.*
>
> *My anxiety returned with a vengeance, when my mother died two years ago. I just fell apart. I began to drink heavily and was arrested for drink driving. I was really worried as I didn't know how I was going to manage looking after my daughter without my Mum's support. I came out in a rash due to my anxiety and I also had trouble sleeping because I was worrying. My husband snores but I dare not wake him up. He says he is a man born to lead and not to follow and needs his sleep to do all of his leadership work that he does at the Fire Station."*

> **What concerns do you have about what Susan said and do you have any follow up questions?**

Susan, tell us about your relationship with your partner?

SECTION 1

Susan describes her relationship:

> "We have been together about 16 years. Although I call Ronald my husband we have never married. He describes weddings as an unnecessary, over lavish expense. We met at college. It's funny, I was recently talking about going back to college to do further studies, but Ronald never let me. We have set roles in our relationship. He is very much the man of the house. He rigidly loves routine and loves every-thing spick and span, and he gets cross if our home gets untidy or if any-thing upsets our routines. I know he gets very cross and shouts at me sometimes but I know he loves me really."

> Does Susan's response to this question cause you any concern? Do you have any follow up questions?
>
> What do you think might be going on in Susan's life?
>
> What impact do you think would there be upon Susan and her life if she were sent to Prison?
>
> What things over Susan's lifetime might have helped her not offend in the first place?
>
> Are there any lifestyle changes do you think Susan could take and if so, what would you recommend she do?

Section 2

Court Report Interview 2

Instructions:
You are at the Probation Office and you are about to interview about Robbie Robinson for the Court Report you are going to write about him and the offence he recently committed.

You first need to read through a summary of the facts of the case and make an assessment of the seriousness of the offence. During the interview, you will give the defendant an opportunity to give their version of the offence and give an explanation for their actions.

You will need to make an assessment of the defendant's truthfulness and willingness to take responsibility for their actions and their level of remorse for what they have done. You need to take account of the victim's perspective of the incident.

You will be making note of Mr Robinson's attitudes, his background and any good and bad points about him.

You are asked to make note of any observations or concerns you might have about his answers.

You will need to consider what follow up questions you would like to ask the defendant.

Facts of the case.
The Police were called to an incident at the Brewery Tap Pub in Axminster at 10.15pm on Saturday 21.10.98. On arrival the Landlord pointed out the defendant, 42- year-old, Robbie Robinson as having assaulted the victim, Timothy Spears. The Landlord said that he had asked the defendant to leave the pub but said Robbie Robinson refused stating "Why should I?"

The Landlord asked the Police remove Mr Robinson and they did so. Mr Robinson left the Pub with the police quietly. When questioned, Mr Robinson stated that the victim's behaviour had provoked him, but that it was a 'fair cop' and that he was sorry for his actions."

Witnesses describe Mr Robinson striking the victim with his fist two or three punches to the victim's head. The victim sustained bruising to his face.

Mr Robinson has two previous convictions for ABH, in similar circumstances, in Public Houses and a conviction for driving with excess alcohol 6 years ago.

> **Having read the above facts of this case what concerns do you have? What follow up questions would you like to ask Mr Robinson?**

The defendant, Robbie Robinson's version of the offence:

"I work hard all week running my firm of plasterers around the building sites. This normally involves long days and early starts I don't do any drinking or go out during the week and so by the weekend I like to go out and enjoy myself.

Any-way, I was standing, with me misses, in this Pub, when this bloke in a flowery shirt kept looking at me. I ignored him at first, but he kept looking and I could swear that he even grinned at me at some point. I thought to myself, I don't know him, is this geezer some sort of poofter or something? And so, I went over and tapped him on the shoulder and asked what's up and he turned his back on me.

Manners don't cost any-thing. Turning his back like to me like that is such a rude thing to do. Well, I can tell you, that really riled me up and so I smacked him one.

But these things happen when a group of lads get together. It's just a way of the world isn't it. Us men routinely knock lumps out of each other at weekends. It just happens round here doesn't it. It is just a way of life.

I'm sorry that it happened though. Usually, I don't need to say or do any-thing. Normally, no words are needed and my presence just speaks for itself."

> **What observations have you about what has been said? What concerns might you have about what Robbie Robinson has said and what follow up questions would you ask him?**

Timothy Spears the victim's account of what happened:

"I was out on a social evening with my colleagues from work when I saw this man on the other side of the pub, who I recognised from somewhere. I was looking at him and racking my brain thinking where did I know him from. Was he one of my friends from the past? I was thinking to myself. He seemed to snarl at me at one point, and then I remembered him, as being a big bully at school and wanted nothing more to do with him, as he regularly went round thumping kids in the school playground.

Any-way, he came over to me, all aggressive-like. It was scary. I really didn't know what to do and then he hit me, three blows to my head with his fists. One blow hit me on the head, behind my ear, one on the side of my forehead and then one on my chin. I lost my balance momentarily, when he hit me on the chin and I almost hit the deck.

It was horrible. I don't know why he did it. This was a totally unprovoked attack on me. My partner John was really upset over the state of me when I got home."

> Having read the victim's account what observations have you about what has been said? What concerns might you have about Robbie Robinson's actions and what follow up questions would you ask him.

What can you tell us about your previous convictions Mr Robinson?

Robbie Robinson tells us about his previous convictions:

> *"My most recent offence was when this bloke in a pub was trying to get far too friendly with my wife and so I hit him one.*
>
> *Then the other assault offence was when this gay guy in a pub seemed to fancy me and so I hit him one so that he'd get the message to leave me alone.*
>
> *After one night's drinking, I was rude to a Policeman once but he soon got over it.*
>
> *I got done for drink driving about six years ago. I was so unlucky to get caught as I can hold my drink and drive really well when I have been drinking. The police only stopped me by chance because they were looking for someone who had just escaped from the local prison. What a disaster, as I got banned for a year and I had to employ one of my lads to drive me around every-where."*

> Do you have any observations about what Mr Robinson said and any follow up questions to ask?

How much do you normally drink Mr Robinson?

Robbie Robinson tells us about his drinking habits:

> "I don't normally drink during the week at all, but I do like to have a good drink at the weekends. During an evening, I normally manage to put away 15 -20 pints of lager without any difficulty. My wife normally acts as my chauffeur, unless there is some kind of emergency."

> Do you have any observations about what Robbie Robinson has said?
>
> Do you have any further questions?
>
> Does Mr Robinson have a physical dependency to alcohol?
>
> Does Mr Robinson have a problem with alcohol, in other words is alcohol contributing to him getting into trouble?

It is apparent that Mr Robinson can function without alcohol and that he is not dependant, upon it.

However, it is apparent that his binge drinking at weekends has contributed to his offending. Such a high level of alcohol intake at the weekends can be risky and possibly harmful to his health.

Tell us about how you got on at school Mr Robinson?

Robbie Robinson tells us about his school days:

> *"Well, I can't say I was particularly academic. I knew that there was always going to be a job for me in my father's plastering business when I left school and so I never really had to apply myself to academic studies. I felt it was all of a bit of a waste of time really. But I did like doing sports really. Keeping fit and building up my body was really important to me you know. I didn't put up with any kid trying to push me around. I took part in all of the sports and was captain of the school basket- ball team."*

> **Do you have any observations about what Robbie Robinson has said? Do you have any follow up questions?**

Tell us about your employment history since you left school Robbie?

Robbie tells us about his employment:

"Well, I even started working in the family plastering business, even when I was at school. I used to do labouring work during the holidays and weekends and loved it. I couldn't wait to leave school and when I did, I started out on the shopfloor as an apprentice. I gradually worked my way up to supervising teams of plasterers and now I've been running the business since my dad, retired six years ago.

We have expanded and grown a lot since I have been in charge. I know the trade inside out and we have won a lot of new contracts and I now have a team of about 30 plasterers on the books. The firm relies heavily on me and won't run without me being there. I therefore make sure every-one has their holidays at the same time as me.

There is a funny tradition in the plastering business. We like to work hard and play hard. After work we all like to have a good drink. In the old days the men used to get paid in cash in the pub at the end of the week and then spend a fair proportion of their wages on booze.

If people had any disagreements they were always quickly sorted out, outside the pub in the carpark. I have a good bunch of men working for me, especially when they apply themselves. We are a good team."

Do you have any observations about what Mr Robinson said? Do you have any follow up

| questions?

Tell us about your home life Mr Robinson?

Robbie Robinson tells us about his home life:

> "Well, I live at home with my wife and two teenage daughters that need to be fed, watered, kept in line and maintained to a high standard like all women do. We live in a three-bedroomed house in a cul-du-sac. My wife works part-time at a firm of accountants and the two girls are in secondary school. I can't complain we have a good life. We normally manage to have a good holiday every year. I normally choose for us to go to Portugal every year."

| Do you have any observations about what Mr Robinson said and any follow up questions to ask?
|
| Prisons can be very violent places involving fights between inmates. How do think Mr Robinson would react and behave to being sent to Prison?
|
| What impact would there be upon Mr Robinson's business if he were sent to Prison?
|
| What impact would there be upon Mr Robinson's family if he were sent to prison?
|
| Do you think any of Mr Robinson's attitudes need

challenging and if so which ones?

Do you think Mr Robinson should consider making any lifestyle changes and if so, what changes do you think he should make?

Section 3

Interview Techniques and Aims of the Court Report Interview

What interview techniques would you use?
Putting the interviewee immediately at ease is so important in my experience. If it was someone's first experience of a court report interview this seemed even more important and to explain the purpose of the report. I used to explain that Probation Service was independent of the prosecution and the defence. I explained the main purpose was to enable the sentencers to know more about the interviewee, their view of their offence and why they committed it, and how they felt about it. It also enabled the Court to know more about the interviewee's background and what was going on in their lives.

We used to avoid using closed questions that resulted in yes or no answers. Much better were open ended questions such as How, What, When, Where.

A rather good technique, that I really liked, was to appear to be totally non -confrontational and not quite always understanding of what had happened. For example, *"I misunderstood the prosecution papers, could you please explain … or draw a picture of what happened so I can understand."*

Another good technique, that worked well, was to repeat the odd word or sentence that the interviewee was saying and to clarify what they were saying. For example, *"If I understand you correctly you are saying that ..."* Repeating the odd word or sentence in our experience conveyed that you were listening to the interviewee and most importantly, had heard and understood, what the interviewee was saying. This in our experience always resulted in the interviewee talking much more openly and in an unprompted way.

At some point during the interview, what had caused the offender to offend would need to be discussed. If there were any contributory factors, these would need to be discussed too. Any previous offences would also need to be discussed, together with any patterns of offending. Getting someone to tell you about the main events in their life, as they were growing up, would often explain how and why they had started offending.

The risk of the offender reoffending would need to be assessed and most importantly, any possible strategies that could be deployed to reduce that risk would need to be discussed.

The Probation Officer would discuss the sentencing options open to the Court with the defendant. The higher the seriousness of the offence, together with the higher the risk posed to the public and together with the higher the likelihood of reoffending would result in a term of imprisonment being considered.

If appropriate, all of the various community options would then be discussed and their suitability for the defendant. If someone had an anger management problem this would then result in a proposal that the defendant complete an Anger Management Programme.

Probation would not only find ways of helping the defendant not reoffend, it would also most importantly put over the victim's perspective of the offence and try to ensure that the defendant understood it.

In addition to this, I was always keen for quite bespoke conditions to be added to someone's sentence. For example, I felt it important that the defendant should pay compensation to the victim for any damage done. I was also keen that the defendant should, if possible, be excluded from going back to where the offence occurred, particularly when violence was involved.

Sometimes offenders needed to work on improving various life skills, such as, literacy, numeracy, social and interpersonal skills. More often than not, the offenders needed to learn how to be more appropriately assertive in their lives.

Once subject to probation supervision, what was exciting for me, was to identify the untapped potential in people and to encourage them to go in a positive direction in their lives. Positive achievements, however big or small were something to be always warmly welcomed.

Section 4

A Violent Offence Committed by a Young Woman

Report 1

Brief Outline of case:

Court Report 1. Crown Court. Defendant Susan Nibbs aged 19 years. Offence ABH.
A normally well- behaved young woman assaults another young woman in a night club over her boyfriend. CCTV shows them fighting, and pulling each other's hair.

Commentary on report 1. How would you sentence Ms Nibbs?
What is society's attitude to female offenders? What was it like for me as a Probation Officer to supervise female offenders?

Instructions:
Imagine you are about to sentence Ms Nibbs.

Carefully read through the following report. It is based upon a real person and real events that actually happened. All of the names of people and places have been changed as have some of the details of the defendant so as to protect their identity.

As you carefully read through the report, think about the facts of the case and what happened. Think about the actions of the victim and the defendant. Think about how the victim of the offence may have been left feeling. Also carefully consider the defendant's behaviour and attitudes and their background.

Once you have read the report proceed onto the *Commentary on Report 1 section* and answer all of the questions before sentencing Ms Nibbs.

Please also give consideration as to what steps society could take towards reducing similar offences happening in future.

THE PROBATION SERVICE

This is a pre-sentence report as defined in Section 3(5) of the Criminal Justice Act 1991, it has been prepared in accordance with the National Standard for pre-sentence reports. It is a confidential document prepared specifically for this court hearing.

HARPERBURY CROWN COURT

Date of Hearing: 10.08.2012

Full name: Susan Nibbs

Address: 33, Rudford Place, Middle Bullingdon, BU 556 7PE

Date of Birth: 27 May 1993
Age 19

Offence and date: ABH (19/10/2011)
Ruttlesford.

Petty sessions area: Ruttlesford

Supervising court: Crown Court

Completion date: 09/08/2011

Report Produced by: Mr John Ebrington

Official title: Probation Officer

Address:
Probation Office, Civic Centre, Ruttlesford Home County. RU 23 8PE

1   **Introduction**

1.1. To prepare this report I have studied the Crown Prosecution Documents for this case and the defendants record of previous convictions. I have held an interview with Ms Nibbs and had a telephone conversation with her family.

2   **Offence Analysis**

2.1. This offence took place at the Qudos Nightclub Ruttlesford, in October 2011. Witnesses describe there being an argument between the victim and the defendant. A fight ensued between the two young women. The victim's hair was pulled and she sustained a 1-2 centimetre cut above her left eyebrow as a result of a glass being put in her face. The victim was taken to hospital where she received six stitches to the cut.

2.2. Ms Nibbs tells me that she was at the Nightclub with her boyfriend and several friends. During the evening, she states she had one glass of wine prior to the incident. Ms Gibbs recalls she felt that there was bad feeling towards her from the victim. This had manifested itself by facial expressions and non-verbal communications at a Public House previously and again at the nightclub. Ms Nibbs says she initially went to confront the victim about it in the nightclub bar area when there was an angry exchange of words. About twenty minutes later, she says the situation escalated following a further heated exchange. She says lost self-control and slapped the victim in the face. This then prompted the victim to strike her back and that they then fought each other by pulling each other's hair.

2.3. Ms Nibbs admits she struck the victim first. She also accepts that the victim sustained a cut to the face. However, she maintains that the cut was not a deliberate act on her part and has no recollection of throwing the glass. Ms Nibbs believes the victim's face may have connected with the glass on the table when she was pulling the victim's hair.

2.4. Ms Nibbs conveys she deeply regrets the incident and states that if given the opportunity she would like to apologise to the victim and explain that she did not intentionally cut her. She admits she would not like to have been cut herself and appreciates the full seriousness of the offence. Although it has not been explicitly said before she believes the argument was in truth over her boyfriend. Ms Nibbs explains that he used to be friendly with the victim and thinks the victim became annoyed with her when she began to form a relationship with him. Ms Nibbs acknowledges that she behaved immaturely, and inappropriately in losing her temper and has since resolved to avoid any confrontations in future.

2.5. Ms Nibbs is a person of previous good character as she has no previous convictions.

3 OFFENDER ASSESSMENT

3.1. Ms Nibbs was born locally and has grown up in Ruttlesford. She is the second eldest in a family of 6 children, ranging from 22 years down to 8 years old. Her mother is a nurse at the District Hospital and her father is a paramedic. Her parents separated about 7 years ago when following difficulties in their relationship her father moved away. Ms Nibbs explains her father has nevertheless kept in contact and regularly visits the children. Ms Nibbs' younger brother who is 12 years old, has a heart condition and this has necessitated him having regular visits to Great Ormond Street Hospital. From what Ms Nibbs tells me, it is apparent that all the children have been brought up to help out with the domestic tasks at home, and to help looking after each other. As Ms Nibbs' elder sister has moved out to her own home and has her own children, Ms Nibbs is the eldest child remaining at home and has responsibilities in look after the other children when her mother is at work. However, she does not seem to find this onerous.

3.2. Ms Nibbs describes having experienced a happy childhood and recalls she enjoyed   being at school. She used to be particularly keen at sports and gained awards in gymnastics before being told to stop practising sports by a hospital consultant following a diagnosis that she had a medical problem with her knees. Ms Nibbs gained good grades in her GCSE's and went on to take a GNVQ in Leisure and Tourism in the sixth form. However, she explains that she became disappointed in the course which seemed to lack focus and decided to leave following finding a job as a cashier in a large pet shop called "Pets are Us" in Ruttlesford. Within a few months she was promoted to the post of supervisor before moving on work with the animals. She was eventually promoted to the post of livestock manager, but says she left after three years, when the firm was taken over by another company and she was made redundant. Currently, she is working as a sales supervisor in a women's clothes shop owned by a large national company. A number of staff are older than her and she explains that she has had to develop good supervisory skills in dealing with them.

4 ASSESSMENT OF THE RISK OF HARM TO THE PUBLIC AND THE LIKELIHOOD OF REOFFENDING.

4.1. Ms Nibbs was extremely polite and courteous in interview when she answered all my questions fully. We discussed at length how this incident came about and how Ms Nibbs might avoid behaving in such an unacceptable way again in future. She made mature and sensible contributions to our discussion. She conveys that the incident has made her more thoughtful and sensitive towards others. She also says she used to have a tendency to speak without thinking, but now is much more careful to think before speaking. Ms Nibbs also says she believes that she had on reflection, felt a bit insecure and that her relationship with her boyfriend was being threatened by the victim, when in reality it really wasn't and that she should have just ignored the victim.

4.2. Ms Nibbs' lifestyle also seems to have changed since the incident. She no longer goes to the Qudos Nightclub and now tends to go out alone with her boyfriend to restaurants or the cinema. On one of the few occasions that she went to Qudos, she says she witnessed a violent incident that made her feel physically sick. This has prompted her not to return there. She now seems happy and confident in her relationship with her boyfriend. Ms Nibbs has given some thought to how she relates to other young women in his company and seems unlikely to behave in such an appalling and immature manner again. Her arrest and the upset it caused her and her family has I have no doubt had a deterrent impact upon her, as has attending Court. She is also concerned that she may lose her job as a result of committing this offence.

4.3. From my discussions with her, it is apparent that she does not normally have an anger management problem or a problem with alcohol or illegal substances. In fact, she expresses strong disapproval of illegal substances stating she feels they are very harmful to individuals and to society. From what she tells me, Ms Nibbs seems to associate with friends who are normal law-abiding individuals. She is a person of previous good character who has no previous experience of coming into contact with the Criminal Justice system. She seems highly motivated towards ensuring that she never has to appear before the Courts again and I accordingly think that there is little risk of her reoffending.

5 CONCLUSION

5.1. The Court will no doubt be taking a serious view of this offence as Ms Gibbs' behaviour in attacking the victim and in cutting her face was wholly unacceptable and could have potentially had much more serious consequences for the victim. The incident appears to have originated from an immature argument between two young women that should have been avoided. Ms Nibbs acknowledges this, expresses genuine regret and seems to have learnt her lesson. I would therefore ask the court not to impose a custodial sentence in this case. Whilst in custody she would be unable to compensate the victim and would be adversely affected by coming into contact with hardened and sophisticated offenders.

5.2. I have discussed Probation with Ms Nibbs and whilst she expresses a willingness to co-operate, I feel that there would be little work to focus on and that such a measure would essentially act as a monitoring exercise. This offence would appear out of character. Overall, Ms Nibbs is a responsible individual and I do not feel that Probation intervention would be of value.

5.3. In my opinion a Community Service Order would suitably punish Ms Nibbs whilst enabling her to repay society constructively by carrying out worthwhile unpaid work for the good of the local community. Ms Nibbs could be banned from going to the Qudos Nightclub. A Compensation Order made out to the victim of her offence would also appear appropriate in this case. I have explained the strict requirements of Community Service to Ms Nibbs and she undertakes to comply.

John Ebrington
Probation Officer

Section 5

Attitudes Towards Women and Crime

Commentary on Court Report 1

What did Ms Nibbs look like?
Ms Nibbs looked like a pleasant young woman. She was neat and tidy and slightly built. She didn't look like someone who is ever violent or aggressive. You could tell that she was nervous and anxious and took her situation seriously. She was attentive in interview and made a good contribution to our discussion.

How did this case get to Crown Court?
It is unusual for a case of ABH (Assault occasioning actual bodily harm) to end up in Crown Court. I really have no idea why it did so. However, I am certain that Ms Nibbs did not ask for it to go for trial at Crown Court. The Court report was not requested as a result of her being found guilty of this offence at Crown Court.

But was her offence really ABH or GBH?
What is GBH? GBH means causing Grievous Bodily Harm to the victim, such as causing broken limbs or a cut or stab wound by using a weapon such as a knife. Other examples of GBH could be attacking someone

with a broken bottle or other dangerous object, such as a hammer. Also kicking someone in the head is a GBH offence, as it causes significantly more risk of serious physical and psychological injury to a person rather than harming them elsewhere. It goes without saying that throwing acid at someone, either in their face or on any other part of their body is always GBH.

GBH section 18 is more serious as it is an offence of intentionally or recklessly causing serious harm to the victim.

The less serious offence of GBH is section 20.

ABH is an offence of causing actual bodily harm. It is less serious than an offence of GBH. Typically, it is an offence that results in any of the following injuries such as bruising, scratches, bite marks, swelling and minor fractures. Causing a small cut can be classified as an ABH.

However, in my opinion an offence involving injuring someone with a glass and causing a cut resulting in 6 stitches, to someone's face would probably normally result in someone being charged with GBH and not ABH, as in this case. It appears to have been a close call in Ms Nibbs' case. Just maybe, possibly, the Crown Prosecution Service took a kindly view of Ms Nibbs and advised she be charged with the lesser charge of ABH.

However, what of the shock horror a young female behaving so violently?

Almost all violent crimes in the UK are committed by men. It is rare for a woman to appear in Court for a violent offence and society is often quite shocked on the rare occasion they do so. It is quite possible that the Magistrates took a very serious view of this offence when they heard of the facts of the case, particularly as it was a female before them, and decided that this case should be sent to the Crown court. The maximum sentence the Magistrates can impose would be six months imprisonment for this offence. By committing this case to Crown Court is a way for the Magistrates to state that they feel they have insufficient powers to sentence the defendant because they feel she deserves more than six months imprisonment for her offence.

> **Do you feel that Ms Nibbs deserves to be sentenced to more than 6 months imprisonment for this offence?**
>
> Yes/No
>
> **How serious is Ms Nibbs' offence?**

Things to be taken into consideration that make a violent offence more serious:

- Little or no remorse for the harm caused to victim and or complete denial of the offence.

- Previous convictions and particularly for similar

offences. Actions that were clearly pre-planned and/or pre-meditated.

- Use of a weapon such as a knife.

- A vulnerable victim.

- Grave injury caused to the victim and significant harm caused to the victim. Significant, permanent scaring to the victim's face.

Things to be taken into consideration that might make the incident possibly a little less serious:

- If the offender has no previous convictions or no relevant/recent convictions.

- A person who displays apparent genuine remorse for their offence.

- If the person is of good character and has previously displayed exemplary conduct in life.

- If there was a significant degree of provocation for the offence.

- If there has been a history of significant violence or abuse towards the offender by the victim.

- If the offender is lacking in maturity and is relatively young.

- If the offender has a mental disorder or learning disability.

- Also, if the offender is the sole or primary carer for dependent relatives.

- If the offender displays genuine determination to address their offending behaviour or has already taken steps to do so.

- If the offender has a serious medical condition that requires urgent, intensive or long-term treatment.

   (If you wish, now go directly to 'Sentencing Ms Nibbs' at the end of this section)

My early experiences of Probation and of working with women

My first introduction to Probation was to do voluntary work with the organisation. I used to help run an evening reporting centre at my local Probation Office, which was situated in a very old former Police station. I recall that they used to keep all of their stationary in the old police cells. Most of the people reporting to the evening centre were men. I recall that used to drive people around in my car to get them to different appointments etc. One young man used slide down the passenger seat in my car, because he felt too embarrassed to be a passenger in a Citroen 2CV car. He didn't want to be seen and lose any of his street credibility.

There was a young woman, who I used to take by car to visit her partner who was serving his sentence in an open prison. Her baby, who had been poorly, used to accompany us on the journey and the object was to enable them to maintain family ties during this difficult time for them.

I then worked part-time as a Community Service Supervisor, supervising offenders doing work on various projects, such as redecorating village halls and tiding up old people's gardens. Women offenders working on these groups were few and far between, but whatever few there were I recall that they were all fine and really good workers. One really lovely project involved redecorating a local community play group centre, where those in charge used to get involved in doing the work with us and motivate us by expressing their genuine appreciation with lots of tea and cake. This really contrasted with a snooty village hall project, where the woman in charge seemed thoroughly condescending, frosty cold and nasty towards us. We didn't feel particularly motivated to work there.

On being promoted to the post of Community Service Officer, responsible for managing all of the Community Service Projects for a local Court area, my manager, who was a female, expressed doubts about my ability to manage female offenders on the Community Service Orders.

I had previously been a manager, in the catering

industry, managing many women without any particular difficulty for over a decade. "Why is that?" I asked her.

"Because I don't think you have met women like that before. They can be very aggressive, difficult, tough and manipulative," she said, leaving me feeling a little apprehensive.

Well, I'm glad to say that I didn't encounter any difficulties with the female offenders. None of them were frighteningly aggressive. Indeed, they were all fine and good to work with. In my experience, you can't stereotype all female offenders as being aggressive, difficult, tough and manipulative. In fact, I found it was often, exactly the opposite. In my experience, nearly every-one has something positive or a skill to offer.

One of the pleasures of the Community Service Officer job, was matching people's skills with the projects. I was quite creative and had ability to think out of the box. I recall placing one really bright young female university student to do work in a Women's refuge, where she did really much needed and worthwhile work. It also proved to be a good learning experience for her and I recall the refuge being really pleased with her work.

There was another young woman, who was a window dresser. I placed her with the Oxfam shop, where she not only did their window displays, but also wrote a manual on how to do window displays for all of their shops. That was greatly appreciated by Oxfam.

I recall another woman, working on a local charitable furniture restoration project, where she really enjoyed doing the work. Some of the women joined the men on the painting and decorating projects and I don't recall any problems with them either.

I was quite successful in the job and my managers encouraged me to apply to go on a university course, in order to train to become a Probation Officer. I'm glad they encouraged me, as I don't think I would have applied otherwise.

When I qualified as a Probation Officer, I first worked in a tough area in London and became experienced in dealing with a high volume of tough crimes. Most of the women I dealt with there were fine. On the whole, the women were mostly victims of crimes and circumstances themselves. They also often lacked in assertiveness skills, self-confidence and self -esteem. There was plenty of positive work that could be done on probation. Many of them also, just needed to move on and learn to say no to the men in their lives.

When my son was born, I moved back to work in my home area, in order to be nearer to home. Having worked in a tough part of London, I seemed much more experienced than many of my colleagues. Following research that suggested that female offenders responded better to female Probation Officers rather than to male ones, it was suggested that all female offenders should only be allocated to female Probation officers.

It was strange, as at my new office, nearly all of my colleagues were female officers, but whenever a female offender needed to be allocated an officer, they were always allocated to me, a male officer. I soon had an awful lot of females on my caseload and never understood why this was the case. However, I'm proud to say most of them stopped offending and some made tremendous progress in their lives, particularly in terms of education and employment.

Sentencing Ms Nibbs

Over to you in Sentencing Ms Nibbs. Having read the report how would you sentence her? But before you do so, please consider the following:

The main things for you to consider are:
a) What is the seriousness of her offence? and
b) What is the risk of her reoffending?

How high is the risk of Ms Nibbs reoffending?

Very low / low / medium / high / very high?

What risk of harm does Ms Nibbs pose the public?

Very low / low / medium / high / very high?

The maximum sentence for ABH is 5 years imprisonment. The minimum sentence is a financial penalty.

A Community Sentence involving probation supervision can be any- thing between 6 months and three years. Attendance to attend offending behaviour groups designed to address issues such as Anger Management can be imposed. Also, Unpaid Work (Community Service) can be imposed for anything between 40 and 300 hours duration.

> **How would you sentence Ms Nibbs?**
>
> **What steps could have possibly been taken during Ms Nibbs's life-time that could have helped her not offend?**
>
> **Would lessons on this sort of topic at school help?**
>
> **What steps could society take to help prevent such violent offending in the future?**
>
> **Why is it that females commit considerably less violent offences than men?**
>
> **What do you think it is like to supervise female offenders?**

Section 6

A Violent Offence Against the Police

Report 2

Brief Outline of case:

Court Report 2. Magistrates Court. Defendant Stuart Ross aged 30 years Offence Assault Police.
Stuart maintains that it was the police who assaulted him and not him the police.

Commentary on report 2. How would you sentence Stuart Ross?
Some of the realities involving Assault Police Officer cases described. The odds of being found 'Not Guilty' of Assault Police in a Magistrates Court is exceptionally low.

Instructions:
Imagine you are about to sentence Mr Ross.

Carefully read through the following report. It is based upon a real person and real events that actually happened. All of the names of people and places have been changed as have some of the details of the defendant so as to protect their identity.

As you carefully read through the report, think about the facts of the case and what happened. Think about the actions of the victims and of the defendant. Also carefully consider the defendant's behaviour and attitudes and their background.

Once you have read the report proceed onto the Commentary on Report 2 section and answer all of the questions before sentencing Mr Ross.

Please also give consideration as to what steps society could take towards reducing similar offences happening in future.

THE PROBATION SERVICE

This is a pre-sentence report as defined in Section 3(5) of the Criminal Justice Act 1991, it has been prepared in accordance with the National Standard for pre-sentence reports. It is a confidential document prepared specifically for this court hearing.

HARPERBURY Magistrates Court

Date of Hearing: 24.08.1999
Full name: Stuart Charles Ross
Address: 59, Old Rudford Place, Bullingdon, BU 556 7PE

Date of Birth: 27 May 1969
age: 30 years

Offence and date: Assault Police 06.05.99
Ruttlesford.

Petty sessions area: Ruttlesford

Supervising court: Ruttlesford

Completion date: 23/08/99

Report Produced by: Mr John Ebrington

Official title: Probation Officer

Address:
Probation Office, Civic Centre, Ruttlesford, Home County. RU 23 8PE

1 Introduction

1.1. I have known Mr Ross since February 1998 when the supervision of his Combination Order was transferred to me. I am also currently supervising Mr Ross on a Probation Order and have had access to his previous probation records. I have received the witness statements and Mr Ross' record of previous convictions from the Crown Prosecution Service. I have held an interview at this office to specifically discuss this case with Mr Ross.

2 Offence Analysis

2.1. It would appear that the incident occurred when the Police were called to Mr Ross' address. The statements suggest that Mr Ross was verbally abusive towards the police, that he spat at one policeman and that he scratched one constable on the neck and kicked another whilst he was being restrained. The seriousness of these offences is heightened by the fact that they were committed whilst Mr Ross was on bail for other matters. Although found guilty of these offences, at the last hearing, Mr Ross still maintains his innocence. He states that he was disappointed to have been found guilty but acknowledges he must now accept the sentence of the Court. As Mr Ross still maintains that he is not guilty I am unable to comment further about these offences.

3 Relevant information about the offender

3.1. Mr Ross appears to have been a prolific offender as a juvenile. Up until he achieved the age of 18 years, he was convicted of numerous offences including theft, taking vehicles without owner's consent, burglary, possession of offensive weapon and arson. During this period, he was sentenced to all available options including lengthy periods in custody. However, since 1991, when Mr Ross was last released from prison there appears to have been a marked decline in Mr Ross' rate of offending. There was a three-year gap before he was convicted again on this occasion for burglary and theft, and a Combination Order was imposed. Records confirm that he satisfactorily completed both elements of the Order.

3.2. Having experienced a chaotic lifestyle during the 1980's which involved alcohol abuse, it seems that Mr Ross used supervision to establish more structure to his lifestyle, cut down on his drinking and resolved his housing problems. He took and passed his driving test for the first time in 1996. Given his history of previous convictions this, was perhaps a significant achievement, which he later spoilt by committing numerous motoring convictions, which resulted in a large number of fines and his disqualification.

3.3. In 1997, he was convicted of driving whilst disqualified and this resulted in him receiving another Combination Order. Mr Ross was initially supervised by another Probation Officer from the Ruttlesford office. However, Mr Ross made a complaint about his supervision and following discussions with the Senior Probation Officer his case was transferred to me in February 1998. Although a good rapport was established with Mr Ross, and he initially reported well, several absences were recorded in July, and all contact was lost with him in August 1998, which then resulted in the Order being returned to Court and a warrant being issued for his arrest. He was eventually arrested and produced at this Court in May 1999, when he pleaded guilty to being in breach of the Order. The Order was revoked and on 20.5.98 Mr Ross was resentenced on the original offences by the imposition of a 12 months- Probation Order with a condition that he attend the 25 + Offending Behaviour group. Community Service was not an option open to the Court because Mr Ross had been certified as being unfit to work following injuries sustained to his hands, which apparently occurred when he was arrested in 1997, when he alleges Police, Officers stamped upon his hands and fractured them.

3.4. At the time of the breach, Mr Ross had left his partner to reside with another woman without notifying Probation of his new address. Mr Ross says that at the time he felt his life was in turmoil, when he felt emotionally torn between two relationships and did not get his priorities right. Since then, he has returned to live with his wife and he says that they have largely overcome their difficulties by setting time aside to talk to each other. His partner tells me that they have also attended Relate. They have two daughters aged 8 years and 3 years and Mr Ross says he regrets that his behaviour had a negative impact on his daughters. Mr Ross conveys that he values being a family man and says that the family now do more activities together, resulting in more harmonious relationships within his family.

3.5. Since the imposition of the new Probation Order, Mr Ross has made good use of supervision to discuss his problems and his previous offending. He has found it frustrating being unable to work, due to the injuries to his hands. During supervision we have discussed other educational and career opportunities which might be open to him.

3.6. I have been in contact with the Court fines office on the telephone and made a list of the information they gave me on the attached page. The total fines, costs, and compensation imposed, amount to some £3,833. In all but one case, which was for an offence of criminal damage, the fines were imposed for traffic offences. The fines office advises me that £1,594 has been paid or remitted to date, leaving £2,238 outstanding. Mr Ross is under the impression that all his fines had been passed to the bailiffs. The fines office advises me that this was previously the case, but that this instruction to the bailiffs, has now been withdrawn. Mr Ross and his family receive £103 per week in income support. I attempted to discuss his outgoings with him, but he seemed very unsure of himself, stating his partner normally manages the family expenditure. I have given him an expenditure chart to complete and have asked him to bring this to Court with him. He acknowledges that he has fallen behind on his payments but states that his family have experienced difficulties in managing their affairs. I do not have details of when Mr Ross last made a payment or how often he has been paying, but I can confirm that I would be willing to supervise a Money Payment Supervision Order if the Court believes that such a measure would assist in this case.

4   Risk to the public of reoffending

4.1. Up until 1992, Mr Ross had a large and appalling record of previous convictions and since then it would appear that he has gained a further three previous convictions, which in its self represents a marked reduction in his criminality. According to his record of previous convictions, he does not have a history of assaults against others, but has a number of previous convictions for criminal damage offences which is of concern. These offences appear to have been drink related. The concerning offence of Arson occurred when he and two other juveniles set fire to the rubbish inside a public bin.

4.2. He tells me that he has never been involved in drug abuse and that his alcohol consumption is currently well under control. He seems motivated to avoid reoffending. Whilst I believe that there is a risk of Mr Ross reoffending, I believe that this is reducing.

5 Conclusion

5.1. Mr Ross has been found guilty of a serious offence which will give cause to consideration of a custodial sentence. I would ask the Court not to take such a course of action as this would have a negative impact on Mr Ross and his family at a time when they have regained some stability.

5.2. Community Service would in my opinion be an appropriate punishment for Mr Ross' unacceptable behaviour. However, he is assessed as unsuitable as he is claiming sickness benefit and has been certified as being unfit to work by his doctor, due to the injuries to his hands.

5.3. Mr Ross was recently made subject of a Probation Order with a condition that he attend an offending behaviour group (details attached). This was following breach and revocation of his Combination Order imposed in 1997. Although far from ideal the Court does have the option of imposing another two-year Probation Order which would in effect extend the period of supervision by another year.

5.4. Regards a Curfew Order, Mr Ross is of a stable address and as far as I am aware he has no regular commitments, which would limit the imposition of such an Order. Although Mr Ross has substantial outstanding fines the Court may wish to consider imposing a Compensation Order to the victims of his offences.

John Ebrington
Probation Officer

Section 7

Assault Police

Case Commentary on Court Report 2

What did Mr Ross look like?
Mr Ross looked a little older than his thirty years. He had an affable, almost apologetic demeanour and seemed to quite enjoy coming to see me, his Probation Officer. He seemed to sometimes have a rueful smile in discussing his previous offending. He would brush his past away, with a sweep of his arm, as if to say that he admitted he was naughty in the past, but that was all history now and that he was now in the business of staying out of trouble.

Can Probation work with someone if they plead not guilty to their offence?
Probation Supervision will not normally be offered if someone maintains they are not guilty of the offence. Why do you think this is?

Why do you think Supervision was offered in this case?
What advantages are there for supervision to be offered?

Anecdotal experiences of Assault Police cases.
In my experience a lot of offenders who claimed that they have been assaulted by the Police were then charged with the offences of assault police. If found guilty of Assault Police you can't claim you have been assaulted by the Police.

Anecdotally, the chances of being found 'Not Guilty' of Assault Police in Magistrates Court trials are incredibly low.

I used to encourage offenders to not allow themselves to get drawn into confrontational situations with the Police Officers. I'd encourage them to rise above losing one's temper with the Police, to remain calm and in control, remain scrupulously polite and to try to understand the police officers' viewpoint too.

I recall one young man as soon as the pubs shut used drive around in a souped- up car, with a really loud exhaust and flashing lights. Why try to draw attention to yourself like that I used to say to him. I also used to encourage offenders to learn skills in being appropriately assertive with people so as to avoid getting into conflict situations.

Sentencing Mr Ross

> What are your experiences of the Police?
>
> What steps over Mr Ross's lifetime could have been taken by society to stop him offending in the way he has?
>
> How high is the risk of Mr Ross reoffending?
>
> Very low / low / medium / high / very high?
>
> What risk of harm does Mr Ross pose the public?
> Very low / low / medium / high / very high?
>
> How would you sentence Mr Ross?

Ross was in fact sentenced to Probation Supervision, as outlined in the report and this was in fact to be the very final occasion he has ever been to Court for a Criminal Offence. He stopped offending altogether.

> Why do you think this was the case?
>
> What do you think could have happened if Ross had been sent to Prison for 12 months?

Section 8

A Victim of Crime Commits an Offence

Report 3

Brief Outline of case:

Court Report 3. Magistrates Court. Defendant Anthony Osbourne aged 26 years.

The offences are Drive with Excess Alcohol and Drive whilst Disqualified. The risk to the public of Driving with Excess Alcohol, whilst disqualified is so high and cannot be understated, and so why is Mr Osbourne behaving this way? Are there any factors that contribute to his offending?

Commentary on report 3. How would you sentence Anthony Osbourne?

Anthony and his family were previously victims of a most traumatic crime which they possibly still have not got over.

Instructions:

Imagine you are about to sentence Mr Osbourne.

Carefully read through the following report. It is

based upon a real person and real events that actually happened. All of the names of people and places have been changed as have some of the details of the defendant so as to protect their identity.

As you carefully read through the report, think about the facts of the case and what happened. Think about the risk posed to potential victims and to the defendant. Also carefully consider the defendant's behaviour and attitudes and their background.

Once you have read the report proceed onto the Commentary on Report 3 section and answer all of the questions before sentencing Mr Osborne.

Please also give consideration as to what steps society could take towards reducing similar offences happening in future.

THE PROBATION SERVICE

This is a pre-sentence report as defined in Section 3(5) of the Criminal Justice Act 1991, it has been prepared in accordance with the National Standard for pre-sentence reports. It is a confidential document prepared specifically for this court hearing.

HARPERBURY Magistrates Court

Date of Hearing: 1.08.1998
Full name: Anthony Osbourne
Address: 26, Catherine Street, Bullingdon, Home County, BU55 7PE

Date of Birth : 7 July 1971
Age : 26 years

Offence and date: Driving with Excess Alcohol
and Driving whilst Disqualified.
Ruttlesford.

Petty sessions area: Ruttlesford

Supervising court: Ruttlesford

Completion date: 31/07/98

Report Produced by: Mr John Ebrington

Official title: Probation Officer

Address:
Probation Office, Civic Centre Ruttlesford Home County. RU23 8PE

1 Introduction

1.1. I have held two office interviews with the defendant during which time we discussed the Crown Prosecution Papers. Mr Osbourne bought with him, as requested by me, documents which confirmed his background details. Although Mr Osbourne has two previous convictions, he has had no previous contact with the Probation Service.

2 Offence Analysis

2.1. The Police were called to an incident at a Petrol filling station in the early hours and subsequently arrested Mr Osbourne for Driving with Excess Alcohol, Driving Whilst Disqualified and No Insurance. He was later found to be at least twice over the legal limit with a reading of 164 ml in his blood.

2.2. Mr Osbourne was originally disqualified in October 1997, about six months before these current offences, for an offence of Driving with Excess Alcohol. On that occasion he was fined £120 and disqualified from driving for 12 months.

2.3. At the time of the current offences, Mr Osbourne was apparently working on a car at his home which he planned to sell at a profit. He says that he had been given the car by a relative and was due to pay for it, once the work was completed and the vehicle sold.

2.4. On the evening in question, Mr Osbourne says that he became tempted to drive the car after having an argument with his girlfriend. He foolishly used the car to go and see a friend. His friend then took him out to a Public House and then on to a nightclub. During the course of the evening Mr Osbourne says he drank at least six vodkas and cokes. At the end of the evening, he recalls driving slowly home and stopped at the petrol station to purchase cigarettes.

2.5. Mr Osbourne makes it plain that he now regrets his actions. He says that he should have asked his friend to drive him home, or even have gone home by taxi. He says that he now feels very stupid to have driven in defiance of a Court ban and to have put other motorists at risk through driving with excess alcohol and without insurance. He feels that there was no excuse for his behaviour and with the benefit of hindsight fully appreciates the full seriousness of his actions. Mr Osbourne tells me that he normally only drinks alcohol occasionally, but did so on this occasion because he was upset and it had clouded his judgement.

3 Relevant information

3.1. Mr Osbourne spent the early part of his life in Southampton where his father had a small business. However, the business encountered financial difficulties and had to be sold when Mr Osborne senior became ill with Parkinsons. The family moved back to London, to be closer to supportive relatives and settled in Wembley where Mr Osbourne went to school.

3.2. Mr Osbourne told me that he had been keen to do well in his exams and go on to a career in engineering and to this end asked one of his teachers for extra tuition. However, he explains that the teacher seemingly became obsessed and infatuated with him, Mr Osbourne and his parents reported this to the education authorities and the teacher was moved to another school. Unfortunately, matters did not end there, but escalated. The teacher concerned, who was apparently mentally unwell, went round to the Osbourne household and painted offensive graffiti on a wall and committed criminal damage to their car. Matters eventually culminated in tragedy, when the teacher again went to the family house with a gun and shot Mr Osbourne and his father, who was killed. As a result of the injuries, he sustained, Mr Osbourne was hospitalised for 11 months. At the time there was widespread media coverage of the incident.

3.3. Mr Osbourne tells me that as a consequence of what happened, he never completed his schooling. He has been actively employed most of his adult life. At the age of 17 years, after he recovered from his physical injuries, he commenced a YTS scheme at a Dry

Cleaners owned by one of his relatives. Mr Osbourne then went on to work at a meat processing factory owned by his uncle, and then went onto to work for another uncle in the garment industry. Latterly, he worked as a "cutter" for another firm in the clothing trade, but tells me he was made redundant about 7 months ago and has been unemployed since.

3.4. Whilst it took a year or so for Mr Osbourne to recover from the physical injuries he sustained from the shooting, it has in fact taken years for him to overcome the mental scars. Mr Osbourne has experienced troubled sleeping, flash backs, and periods of depression. He explains that it was fortunate that his employers were, for the most part, supportive relatives who were understanding if he occasionally took time off work as a result of his depression. Mr Osbourne blamed himself for his father's death and was referred to a psychiatrist in 1996 who diagnosed him as being clinically depressed. He was apparently offered counselling but declined to attend, when he says he felt out of place. It is apparent that Mr Osbourne has attempted to get over the incident by his own efforts; from what he tells me, although he has been offered medication in the past, he declined being prescribed drugs, as he feared becoming dependent upon them. It is also apparent that he has never undergone any form of counselling since the incident.

3.5. Mr Osbourne's mother lives in Bronte, where he

lived with her until about six months ago. He has now moved into a small flat in Wembley where he lives on his own.

3.6. He currently is in receipt of £50.50 per week Job Seekers Allowance. According to Mr. Osbourne his weekly out goings are as follows: rent £15.00 per week, groceries £15.00 per week electricity £5.00 per week gas £ 2.00 per week bus fares £5.00 per week cigarettes £6.00 per week

3.7. Mr Osbourne has known his girlfriend for about 10 months. He says they plan to settle down together and plan to eventually get married. He explains that apart from his relationship with her, he feels that he leads a boring existence and that his life is "in a rut ". He recalls that on the evening the offences occurred he was looking forward to going out with his girlfriend, as they rarely are able to go out together, because she frequently works in the evenings. However, she said she felt too tired to go out and he became frustrated and began arguing with her. He now feels that he was extremely stupid to have allowed himself to be upset and behave in a manner which led up to these offences. Mr Osbourne is awaiting a claim from the Criminal Compensation Board. He tells me that he has to date received an interim payment of £5, 000 and is awaiting a final decision on the 26.07.2000. He has been advised that the final award may be substantial. He has no clear plans about what he might do with the money, but is thinking about setting up a small catering business for his girlfriend to manage.

4 Risk to the public of reoffending

4.1. Mr Osbourne does not present as being a particularly aggressive individual who would set out with the deliberate intention of harming the public. However, by drink driving and by driving whilst disqualified he has put other road users and himself at risk. The fact that he has two convictions for Driving with Excess Alcohol, and latterly with such a high reading, does raise concerns that he may have a drink problem. From what he tells me he normally only drinks moderately but drank to excess prior to the offence when he was upset. However, in my opinion using alcohol as a prop when faced with emotional problems can sometimes lead to dependency. I believe that Mr Osbourne would benefit greatly from the Alcohol Related Offenders Programme and that such a measure would reduce the risk of reoffending in future.

4.2. Mr Osbourne has been through a most tragic experience in the past, but he does not seek to use it as an excuse for his offending behaviour. However, what is of concern to me, is that Mr Osbourne seems to be leading a fairly aimless existence with few purposeful activities and is possibly too dependent on his girlfriend. He seems to be a person of low self-esteem and at times he may still be suffering from depression. Mr Osbourne has never received any form of counselling since the incident and Probation could make arrangements for him to have access to this. Probation would also encourage Mr Osbourne to take up new activities. For example, he could be encouraged to possibly do voluntary work for victim support and to explore the various educational, training and employment opportunities which may be open to him. Mr Osbourne said that he would very much welcome this. He seems motivated ensure that he does not re-offend and assures me that he will not have anything to do with cars in future whilst subject to a ban.

5 Conclusion

5.1. Driving whilst disqualified, and whilst under the influence, often result in the imposition of custodial sentences. However, I would ask the Court not to follow such a course of action on this occasion as I believe that such a measure would have a wholly negative impact on Mr Osbourne.

5.2. Mr Osbourne is assessed suitable for a Curfew Order and I have explained to him what such an Order entails. However, this not my preferred option in this case as I understand his accommodation is about to be refurbished which would require him to live temporarily with his mother, who is not aware of the offences.

5.3. Mr Osbourne is also assessed suitable for a Community Service Order, be it an Order in its own right, or as part of Combination Order. Such an option would suitably punish Mr Osbourne and would enable him to repay society in a constructive manner.

5.4. However, I propose Mr Osbourne be made subject to a Probation Order with a condition that he attend the Alcohol Related Offenders Programme. The aims of individual supervision would be to:

5.5. Supervise him strictly in accordance with National standards for community Sentences. Monitor his future behaviour.

5.6. Encourage him to take up purposeful activities. Give him practical assistance and advice into employment.

5.7. Provide him with a forum to discuss his problems and to assist him to clarify his future plans.

5.8. Make arrangements for him to be offered bereavement counselling.

Mr John Ebrington
Probation Office

Section 9

Life Experiences can Undoubtably Contribute to Becoming an Offender

Case Commentary on Court Report 3

All walks of life
People come from all walks of life for their Court Report interview with the Probation Officer. I recall in one case a woman had become anxious over the potential release from prison of her father. This anxiety had contributed to her drink driving. When she was aged 15, her father had raped her and made her pregnant resulting in her having to have an abortion. To make matters worse, her mother had kept the incident secret and the young woman became an outcast from the family. She left home and made a difficult and unsupported start into adulthood and independent living. However, she later decided to reconcile with her family when she herself had a daughter.

When her daughter became 14 years, her father did the same to her daughter and the matter came out when her daughter was referred for counselling with a psychologist. Her father was then prosecuted for both offences against both women and sentenced to a term of imprisonment.

Probation officers normally have no knowledge of people's backgrounds before they come for interview and so require quite a lot of skill in putting people at ease and in interviewing them. Trauma in people's lives can, it seems, sometimes contribute to people getting into trouble in some way or other and it is not something that is easy to talk about.

One sad case, I recall, involved a young man who was living with his father who was terminally ill and about to pass away. There were just the two of them in the house and the psychological pressure upon the young man was just tremendous. Depressed and fed up of his circumstances the young man went out one night and stole a camper van. His aim was to get away from it all and live by the seaside in the camper van. Only he did not get very far, as the van broke down on a busy roundabout and he was caught by the police who had come to his rescue.

Sentencing Mr Osbourne

What did Mr Osbourne look like?
He had dark hair and was casually dressed. He seemed quiet and respectful. He answered all of the questions put to him openly and fully.

> **What steps would you take, in order to put people at ease for a Court Report interview?**
>
> **How high is the risk of Mr Osbourne reoffending?**
>
> Very low / low / medium / high / very high?
>
> **What risk of harm does Mr Osbourne pose the public?**
>
> Very low / low / medium / high / very high?
>
> **What would you sentence Mr Osbourne to?**
>
> **What steps do think society could have taken that would have possibly helped Mr Osbourne to not have become an offender in the first place?**

Section 10

The Case of a Persistent Sex Offender

Report 4

Brief Outline of case:

Court Report 4 has been prepared for Crown Court.
The defendant is Stuart Cain who is aged 60. He has committed an offence of Gross Indecency with a child aged 14 years. Stuart Cain has been a sex offender for many years and has never completed a Sex Offender Programme designed to address this type of offending.

Commentary:
I describe what was it like for me to work with Sex Offenders. I also describe some of the steps that are taken to protect the public from Sex Offenders.

Instructions:
Imagine you are about to sentence Mr Caine.

Carefully read through the following report. It is based upon a real person and real events that actually happened. All of the names of people and places have been changed as have some of the details of the defendant so as to protect their identity.

As you carefully read through the report, think about the facts of the case and what happened. Think about the risk posed to potential victims and to the defendant. Also carefully consider the defendant's behaviour and attitudes and their background.

Once you have read the report proceed onto the Commentary on Report 4 section and answer all of the questions before sentencing Mr Caine.

Please also give consideration as to what steps society could take towards reducing similar offences happening in future.

THE PROBATION SERVICE

This is a pre-sentence report as defined in Section 3(5) of the Criminal Justice Act 1991, it has been prepared in accordance with the National Standard for pre-sentence reports. It is a confidential document prepared specifically for this court hearing.

HARPERBURY Crown Court

Date of Hearing: 11.05.2000

Full name: Steven CAIRN
Address: 26, College Street, Bullingdon, Home County, BU56 7PE

Date of Birth : 22/03/1940
age : 60 years

Offence and date: Gross Indecency with a child
(Girl aged 14 years)

Petty sessions area: Ruttlesford

Supervising court: Ruttlesford

Completion date: 10/05/2000

Report Produced by: Mr John Ebrington

Official title: Probation Officer

Address:
Probation Office, Civic Centre Ruttlesford Home County. RU23 8PE

1 Introduction

1.1. To prepare this report I have received papers from the Crown Prosecution Service and a list list of previous convictions. I have held one interview with the defendant at HMP Brookhall, I have seen Probation Service records about previous periods of supervision. I have conducted a standard screening for basic literacy and numeracy skills. I have seen the minutes from the local Area Risk Panel meeting, which included information from the police and the local Mental Health Team concerning the defendant.

2 Offence analysis

2.1. The defendant is a 60- year- old man who is before the Court for an offence of Gross Indecency with a 14 -year -old girl. Mr Cairn has been remanded in custody, which reflects the gravity of this offence. He has a lengthy list of previous convictions that include some 9 sexual offences. In discussing this with the defendant, he appears to be under no illusions over the serious nature of his offence and that he is at risk of being sentenced to a term of imprisonment.

2.2. This offence occurred earlier this year and took some time to come to the attention of the police. The victim cannot recall exactly when it occurred. On the day of the offence, she said that she drank some wine with some friends, who were also aged

14 years. She said that they then decided to go round to the defendant's home where they said they knew they could obtain money by offering the defendant sexual services. The victim's two friends stayed outside whilst she went inside the defendant's house. He then asked her to masturbate him, which she did and he then paid her £40 before she left.

2.3. The defendant initially denied the offence to the police, stating he was impotent and that the girls had come round to sell a phone on an earlier date. Several hours later following his remand in custody he then made a full admission of his guilt. He said that the offence had arisen as a result of previous conversations he had exchanged with them at a market stall that he helped run in Hunterbury Town Centre.

2.4. Mr Cairn told me that his recollection is that the offence occurred in April this year. He told me that he took full responsibility for his offence and deeply regretted his actions. Although he told me that he had experienced mental health problems in the past, he asserted that he was quite sure that this current offence did not have anything to do with mental health issues. He conveyed that he had striven hard to re-establish himself back in the community and had not only let himself down, but had also let down the Probation and Police Officers who had been working with him.

2.5. The defendant advised me that the offence had occurred at a time when he was experiencing difficulties with his partner. He said that he had an episode of impotency problems and that she had temporarily ended the relationship following showing her insufficient attention.

2.6. He states that he initially made friends with the young girls, as they were friends of a young man who used to occasionally help him on his market stall. He maintains that the girls were aware that his partner had temporarily ended their relationship. His account is that they used to tease him and had suggested to him that he may perhaps need to seek sexual attentions or services elsewhere. This in my view is distortion on his part and an attempt to shift any responsibility.

2.7. Mr Cairn told me that he initially felt intrigued by the young girl's attention, when she called round and he said that he should have dealt with the situation much better by asking her age. He told me he had foolishly assumed that she was above the age of consent. He told me that he felt flattered by the girl's attention and that she may be interested in someone his age. He told me that if only she had been slightly older, he would not have got into trouble. He said he felt shocked when he found out her true age. He told me that he had no contact with the victim since and I am aware that she confirms this in her statement.

2.8. The defendant's actions were clearly pre-meditated. He was a mature man who was significantly older than the three 14- year- olds. From his own account he allowed himself to get over friendly with them and allowed conversations to involve sexual innuendo. Clearly, in view of his age, he should have had a much greater sense of responsibility towards the girls and distanced himself, particularly, in the light of his previous convictions. Given his account of his discussions with the three girls it is, in my view apparent, that he felt sexually attracted towards them and that he enticed them. In discussing this with Mr Cairn, he conveyed that he understood the concept of grooming victims for sexual offences, but denied this having taken place. It is plain that the victim had gone round with the clear idea that she could obtain money from him by offering sexual services. Although he told me that he had felt "sad and sorry" for the victim, this seems at odds with his subsequent statement that he had felt quite "flattered to have pulled such an attractive young lady." From this, I got the impression that he may have thought that she may have got some sort sexual enjoyment out of the incident and that he had little concept of the power imbalance between them and just how soiled and degraded victims often feel in such situations.

2.9. In my opinion, this offence occurred because Mr Cairn has deviant and distorted thinking processes, poor insight into women's perspectives and poor victim empathy and that these were all contributary factors to this offence.

3 Offender Assessment.

3.1. The defendant's first sexual offence occurred in 1961, when at the age of 18 years he was convicted of Indecent Exposure. There then followed four further Indecent Exposure convictions, plus two other similar offences taken into consideration, between 1961 and 1965. There then followed a gap before he was next convicted for two offences of Indecent Exposure in 1972. In 1980, he was convicted for Obtaining Property by Deception and an offence of ABH. I understand that the victim of the assault was a man. There was then a 16-year gap before he was convicted at this Court in 1996 for the most worrying offence of taking a nine-year-old child without lawful consent and gross indecency towards her and I go into this offence in greater detail later in this report. As a general comment about Mr Cairn's offending, I form the view without wishing to mitigate the seriousness of his actions in any way, that his offences appear to have occurred at stressful periods in his life. It is perhaps significant that he was in a happy and settled relationship during the 16-year gap in his offending.

3.2. The defendant's early formative experiences are important in my view. From his account, his father was a negative role model, as he described him as being a womaniser and as being abusive towards his mother and himself. He told the psychiatrist, Dr Sachs who prepared his report in 1996, that he recalled his childhood as being stressful as his mother had frequently rowed with his father. He conveyed to the psychiatrist that as a child, he had not appreciated his mother's view point and had felt angry with her for arguing with his father.

3.3. No records exist about the details of the early Indecent Exposure offences. What he told me was in congruence with what he told Dr Sachs in 1996, that all the offences apart from one offence in 1965, involved victims who were middle-aged women. The victim in 1965 was he said aged approximately 16 years. From his account all the offences followed a similar pattern of events and actions. His description of a typical Indecent Exposure offence was that it would occur in daylight. He claims that he would have a flaccid penis and that he would not masturbate at the scene or later. The background to the offences typically involved his having experienced an argument with a woman or having felt humiliated by a woman in a superior position.

3.4. His motivation to expose, he claimed, was to shock and embarrass the victim in the hope, that the female selected at random would be upset. On one occasion the offence was apparently due to him having been reprimanded by a female supervisor at work. On another, he had been upset by a woman who had honoured a cheque and on another he had a disagreement with his wife.

3.5. Mr Cairn denies having ever previously used prostitutes or of ever having been interested in deviant sexual practices. He describes himself as always having been heterosexual and states that he usually finds young women aged in their twenties and early thirties attractive. He denied finding young girls or girls in school uniforms attractive - l somehow doubt this. He met and married his wife when he was aged 22 years and she was 16 years. The fact that she was 16 years may nevertheless perhaps be significant.

3.6. Mr Cairn's father died when Mr Cairn was aged 21 years and this appears to have had a stressful impact upon him. He unsuccessfully tried to take over and manage his father's furniture business for a while and his first Incident Exposure offences occurred at this time. They continued even though he was newly married, but from his account the offences seemed to occur when faced with stressful circumstances. When faced with difficulties it is apparent that he has reacted wholly inappropriately by the commission of these sexual offences, for which he must take full responsibility.

3.7. During the 16-year gap that no sexual convictions occurred, he was as previously stated, in a happy and settled relationship with his partner. For about

12 years of this from his account he was a Driving Instructor and no sexual convictions occurred during this period. However, he did explain that he was convicted of obtaining property by deception which had involved him taking people's money and then not giving them driving lessons.

3.8. The 1996 conviction seems to have occurred when the defendant had been experiencing relationship difficulties with his partner. The victim of the offence was a nine -year- old girl who had learning difficulties, which in my view is deeply distressing given the vulnerability of the poor victim. Mr Cairn was found guilty following a trial at this Court. He took the girl in his car to a secluded wood and exposed himself to her. A witness saw him take her to a sweet shop and the victim said that she had been offered sweets and money by him. This leaves me with concerns that there are disturbing parallels between this previous offence and his current offence, which he appears to fail to recognise.

3.9. Although he subsequently admitted the offence, he maintained that he had not enticed the young girl into his car and that he had taken her in the car because he had been pestered by her to do so. He also suggested to me that he had exposed himself to her because she had pestered him. The Probation Service noted that on passing sentence Judge Polston made the following comment, "When arrested you sought to blame the problem on the little girl. You sought to say to those who prepared the reports on you, that you acted this way as the little girl pestered you. I reject that, I say you as the adult were responsible, not the little girl."

3.10. At the time of sentencing Dr Sachs stated in his psychiatric report that his assessment was that the defendant was not mentally ill and specifically stated that Mr Cairn did not suffer with depression or any kind of schizophrenia. However, the apparent onset of schizophrenia in prison prevented him from fully completing the Sex Offender Treatment Programme over the course of his sentence. Following release, he started the course again but an apparent re-occurrence meant that he left the programme again. Records confirm that he otherwise reported satisfactorily as instructed to his supervising officer and kept his psychiatric appointments. Supervision appears to have focussed upon assisting him re- establish himself back into society and in conjunction with the other services, such as the Police and the Mental Health Unit in monitoring his circumstances. He appears to have used supervision appropriately to discuss strategies to deal with issues that were concerning him. He was open in confiding that he had been experiencing impotency problems over a number of years. He befriended a woman at an outpatient's club for people with mental health issues and they formed a settled relationship together. Given her potential vulnerability the situation was monitored and supervision provided a good forum to resolve any relationship difficulties. His period of supervision ended in July 1999 as did his sentence.

3.11. Mr Cairn advises me he that he has been in receipt of sickness benefit due to his mental health problems. He told me that he has loans and debts in the region on £40,000. This was apparently to purchase a car and material items for his home and he told me that he had felt confident in his ability to repay the money. It is worrying that he took out such large loans when on a low income and I frankly doubt his ability to repay them. Representatives of the Mental Health Unit recently advised the Local Area Risk Panel that their assessment was that Mr Cairn does not have a diagnosis of schizophrenia. They expressed the view that he has depressions and some elements of paranoia, but an insufficient diagnosis to have been a concern.

4 Assessment of the Risk of Harm to the Public and Likelihood of Reoffending

4.1. This offence involved a power imbalance and a young girl who was the victim. His attitude to this offence and his previous 1996 offence leaves me with grave concerns. He has poor victim awareness. He has a tendency to blame the victims of his offences and to justify his own behaviour. He does not appear to have addressed his offence that he committed in 1996 or to have taken full responsibility for it. He has never completed the Sex Offender Treatment Programme and therefore has never addressed the underlying reasons for his offending. Using the Risk Matrix 2000 assessment tool, he has been assessed as being at high risk of reoffending.

4.2. Given the defendant's previous history, it would seem reasonable to conclude that he poses a risk to the public and in particular to all women. The most likely offences are gross indecency and exposing himself. It is hard to predict what he is likely to do in the future.

4.3. However, he was polite and cooperative in interview. He appeared willing to discuss his offending behaviour and seemed open to being challenged on occasion. He said he would be agreeable to undertake a Sex Offender Treatment Programme and told me there were no barriers to him being able to comply on this occasion. He seemed eager to convey that he would be keen to cooperate with the Probation Service as alternative to custody.

4.4. There are no indications that the defendant is at risk of self- harm. However, having spoken with the Police they indicated concerns about the local community's reaction to his offence.

5 Conclusion

5.1. This is an offence of grave concern, particularly

in the light of the defendant's record of previous convictions and the assessment that he would appear to be at high risk of re- offending. Given this, the Court will be seriously considering the imposition of a custodial sentence in this case. Should the Court impose a custodial sentence, I would recommend an extended period of supervision as outlined by sec 85 of the powers of the Criminal Courts Act (sentencing 2000) and this would need to be for a period of three years to ensure completion of the Community Sex Offender Programme.

5.2. In the unlikely event of the Court being willing to consider an alternative to custody, I would propose that Mr Cairn be made subject to a three- year Community Sex Offender Programme as I believe it offers the Court a constructive opportunity to address his offending behaviour.

John Ebrington
Probation Officer

Section 11

Trying to Protect the Public from Sex Offenders

Case Commentary on Court Report 4

A lot goes into a report
As you can see quite a lot of work goes into writing a Court Report. This is a long and detailed report that looks at the defendant's history of his offending and his possible reasons for it.

The report is not only just useful for the Court sentencing, it is also useful for those who will be those supervising Mr Caine in the future. It will give them pointers on what needs to be challenged and addressed.

Not so straightforward to deal with
Sex offenders can be the least straightforward and most difficult people to deal with for Probation Officers. Complete denial that anything actually occurred is not uncommon, particularly at the beginning of a case. Getting them to be open and honest about what they have done is important in working with them to stop offending. Getting them to see and understand the victims' perspectives and to empathise with the victims'

feelings is, I feel, so important.

Sometimes emotionally draining and upsetting
The offences can be really emotionally draining and upsetting to deal with too. I recall one offence where the offender was skilfully manipulative in getting you to feel sorry for them. I then felt totally at odds with this when, I met the young female victim who was so visibly, physically and emotionally, distressed by the offences.

Possibly something went wrong in their formative years
Invariably, something seems to have gone wrong in these offenders' childhoods as they were growing up, that has contributed to them becoming offenders. It seems in Mr Caine's case that it was during his early formative years, that he developed his inappropriate and negative attitudes towards women.

Only the most experienced tended to deal with them
When I was in the Probation Service, sex offenders tended to be dealt with by a specialist team of experienced Officers, who were in receipt of specialist training for the job. I only rarely dealt with Sex Offenders, as I tended to specialise in prolific offenders, people with drug and alcohol offences and persistent offenders over my career. My main skill set was to motivate people to go in positive directions in life and to help and encourage them to do so. Working with Sex Offenders was all about monitoring and containing the risk the offender posed to the public and hopefully

reducing it. I didn't deal with sex offenders too often, but of the few occasions that I did, they were quite memorable.

Some of the most memorable Sex Offender cases I ever dealt with

Sometimes, the sex offenders' offences honestly seem quite laughably bizarre and weirdly funny. I recall one man, accused of indecent exposure telling me, *"But I was only having a pee behind a tree in the woods when the woman saw me"*.

To which, I replied, *"But what were you doing in the woods with the top half of your body dressed in an underwater frogman's outfit, and the lower part of your body totally naked? You also had a magic wand in your hand pointing at your penis. Why was that?"*

Sometimes, we were required to see people that were being supervised by a colleague who was off sick. I recall one man, who was a well to do estate agent, who came into my office looking incredibly respectable and very smartly dressed. I remember he was balding and had a very shiny head. I almost thought that he was one of our respectable middle-class magistrates coming to visit me. I was then taken a bit aback, as I had never heard of people doing such a thing before, but I discovered from his papers, he had been on the underground, furtively, trying to look up women's skirts with a mirror attached to his shoe. I think he had experienced pretty much his entire childhood in rather unpleasant boys boarding schools and regarded women as intriguingly strange alien objects to be approached with a mirror on his shoe. I really don't rate his chances of forming positive relationships in life.

Then there was another man, who used to go to all of the film premieres in Leicester Square and who had left all of his female victims feeling quite bemused and perplexed, when they discovered something quite wet and sticky on their clothing covering their rears.

The other activity he used to do, was to secretly record women's bottoms, going up the London Underground escalators by using a camera hidden in his sports bag. He would then use the images for his own purposes when he reviewed them at home.

There was another strange man, who used to keep dashing into the women's toilets in the local supermarkets. He couldn't really deny doing this, as he had been caught on numerous occasions on the shops CCTV systems. It's sad to say that he got his excitement from illicitly sniffing the women's toilet seats.

Sorry, I know that it feels awkward and embarrassing to discuss these sorts of cases, but some-how we as a society need to find ways of reducing this sort of behaviour both from happening in the first place, but also from reoccurring once they have happened. In my experience, the Sex Offender Programmes do have a good record in significantly reducing these offences from reoccurring.

Something seems to be going wrong in the way some people are growing up. Certainly, there is a discussion to be had about improving people's formative years, about equipping people with better empathy skills and learning to treat people with equal respect and as human beings, with feelings and not as objects in my view. We also need to help victims to become more assertive in dealing with all the inappropriate sex-texting and requests, that goes on amongst young people. We all need to assertively say no more of this thank you.

People probably don't realise that quite a lot can go on behind the scenes in order to protect the Public.
The Police in our area had a small dedicated team of police officers who worked closely with us in Probation in order to supervise serious sex offenders upon their releases from Prison. The releases were done very quietly and discretely without the general public noticing.

I recall supervising a most serious sex offender on his release from prison following serving a custodial sentence for having committed serious sexual offences against 14 -year- old boys.

We started putting in place steps to protect the public before his release. In the Probation files we had records of all his previous offences, assessments and reports about him going back many years. There were also very interesting copies of correspondence between himself and his late mother and other relatives that were all very revealing. Copies of all of these documents were sent to a specialist psychologist, who made a detailed study of them and following this, assessed the offender as being at high risk of reoffending.

A multi-agency risk panel meeting was held which set out detailed plans for his release in order to protect the public. Specific conditions were added to his prison licence which he had to adhere to, during the period of his licence. These included living at a specific address every night. He was not permitted to enter any public parks or play areas, or to approach any children. As well as being required to attend appointments, with the police and probation, he also had to attend for appointments, when he was to be submitted to lie detector tests.

Our aim was to protect the public, but also to help him lawfully re-integrate back into society. We carefully checked his proposed release address to check that it was as safe as possible to the public. We made sure that it was nowhere near any public play areas or schools and the like or over- looking any private gardens where children might be playing.

Part of our job was also to be quiet and discrete about his release and not heighten any risk of violent reactions from the general public.

His address in a block of flats was carefully vetted and a covert camera was installed in the hallway to watch his comings and goings. A bugging device was also installed on his car. His movements were also plotted from the use of his mobile phone.

To cut a long story short, a serious offence was committed in a nearby town and he was suspected of committing it. However, there was insufficient evidence to issue a warrant for his arrest.

However, his surveillance was immediately stepped up and the police followed him into a public play park, carparking area, where he sat watching children in his car. The police arrested him for being in breach of his prison licence and inside his car they found sweets, rope and a balaclava. Basically, because the Probation Service had asked for the condition not to enter parks, to be put on his prison licence, this had enabled the Police to arrest him for the breach and for him to be returned to Prison.

The public probably don't appreciate all of the work that can go on behind the scenes in order to protect them. Instead, people tend to only hear of things when they go wrong.

Sentencing Mr Caine

What did Mr Caine look like?
He has quite a small stature for a man. You could see that he was a man in his sixties. He had blue eyes and a balding head. He had a white beard and looked a bit like a kindly father Christmas. He seemed quite eager to please but tended to look away and have poor eye contact with you on occasion.

> **For whatever reason Mr Caine has never completed a Sex Offender Programme. Why was this?**
>
> **What events in his childhood do you think could have contributed to him becoming an offender?**
>
> **Do you think he is accepting all responsibility for his offences?**
>
> **How high is the risk of Mr Caine reoffending?**
>
> Very low / low / medium / high / very high?
>
> **What risk of harm does Mr Caine pose the public?**
>
> Very low / low / medium / high / very high?
>
> **How would you Sentence Mr Caine?**

What work and support do you think should be given to the victim in this case?

What could we do as a society to reduce similar crimes from happening in future?

Section 12

Many Offenders Start Offending as Children

Report 5

Brief Outline of case:

Court Report 5: has been prepared for Magistrates Court.
The defendant is Simon Long who is aged 18 years. His offence is 'Take a vehicle without owners' consent.'

Simon Long began offending as a child when he stopped attending school. He then became a prolific offender when he abused drugs

Commentary:
Many young people start offending after giving up attending school. How can we as a society stop this from happening?

Instructions:
Imagine you are about to sentence Mr Long.

Carefully read through the following report. It is based upon a real person and real events that actually

happened. All of the names of people and places have been changed as have some of the details of the defendant so as to protect their identity.

As you carefully read through the report, think about the facts of the case and what happened. Think about the risk posed to potential victims and to the defendant. Also carefully consider the defendant's behaviour and attitudes and their background.

Once you have read the report proceed onto the Commentary on Report 5 section and answer all of the questions before sentencing Mr Long.

Please also give consideration as to what steps society could take towards reducing similar offences happening in future.

SECTION 12

THE PROBATION SERVICE

This is a pre-sentence report as defined in Section 3(5) of the Criminal Justice Act 1991, it has been prepared in accordance with the National Standard for pre-sentence reports. It is a confidential document prepared specifically for this court hearing.

HARPERBURY Magistrates Court

Date of Hearing: 1.05. 1998

Full name: Simon LONG
Address: No Fixed Abode

Date of Birth: 16/08/1979
Age: 18 years

Offence and date: Take a vehicle without owner's consent
Drive whilst Disqualified
12.02.1998

Petty sessions area: Ruttlesford

Supervising court: Ruttlesford

Completion date: 30/04/1998

Report Produced by: Mr John Ebrington
Official title: Probation Officer

Address:
Probation Office, Civic Centre Ruttlesford Home County. RU23 8P

1 Introduction

1.1. This report is based upon my knowledge of Mr Long since I commenced supervising him on his Young Offender Licence following his move to this area in December 1997. I have discussed these offences with Mr Long during the course of normal supervision and he has also attended an interview to specifically discuss his case in detail with me. I have read the witness statements from the Crown Prosecution Service, but unfortunately, I have not been sent his record of previous convictions. I have read his probation records sent to me from Derbyshire.

2 Offence Analysis

2.1. Mr Long gives a very confused account of his offence. He states that he was very intoxicated at the time and he says that he is unsure what exactly happened. Despite this he makes it clear that he now feels ashamed to find himself at Court, as he says he has let himself down after deciding to stay out of trouble when he left custody in November 1997.

2.2. From the witness statements, it would appear that Mr Long walked by a parked van, then for whatever reason, suddenly got in it and tried to start it. Several people tried to stop him whilst the van moved forwards a short distance, before he was restrained by an individual. Mr Long thinks he was trying to get away from people who he believed were attacking him, but when pressed he seems unsure and confused. All the witnesses confirm that Mr Long seemed rather intoxicated and the Police waited until the next day to interview him.

2.3. Mr Long says he wishes to apologise to the victims and the Court for his offence and for his bad language and behaviour before his arrest.

3 Relevant information about the offender

3.1. Mr Long describes a happy childhood in Westfield until his family moved to Derby when was aged about 11 years old. Once there, his family had difficulty in adapting to life in Derbyshire, where he says people from London were treated as outsiders.

3.2. According to Mr Long, his father was very strict at home and insisted that he spent hours practising his football skills. There was little scope for fun or contact with his friends whilst at home and he believes that this may have contributed to him becoming a bit over boisterous, whilst he was at his new Primary school.

3.3. Mr Long's transition into the local secondary school went very poorly. He said he hated it and stopped going altogether after a few days. He recounts he spent most of his time truanting, with another child who had also recently moved to the area from London. His failure to attend school does not appear to have been followed up by the school and the local authorities as no contact was made with his parents, who were apparently unaware of his failures to attend school.

3.4. Mr Long committed his first offence aged 12 years old with his truanting friend. They broke into a house, where they spent several hours watching television and consumed items from the fridge, before leaving without taking any other property with them.

3.5. By the time he was 14 years old, his parents had lost all control over him and he became involved with other older young people, who abused alcohol and experimented in drugs. For a short while, he was sent by Social Services to stay with foster parents, in order to give his parents some respite support. Despite the intervention of Social Services, he became addicted to crack cocaine and built-up considerable debts, to those who had supplied him with drugs. He then began to commit numerous offences to pay off his debts. With the benefit of hind-sight, he now says that he is ashamed of his offending behaviour. He tells me he was encouraged by the criminals to whom he owed money, to supply drugs to others, as a way of clearing his debts, but instead of doing this, he used the drugs himself resulting, in him getting into serious trouble with those who had supplied him.

3.6. In February 1996, when he was 16 years old, he was sentenced to custody for the first time, for offences of burglary and theft, and for a breach of an Attendance Centre Order. Whilst in Youth Custody, he developed an addiction to heroin. After his release, his offending behaviour worsened and in February 1997, at the age of 17 years, he was convicted of Burglary offences, Aggravated Taking a Vehicle without owner's consent and Driving whilst Disqualified. A hundred and seventy-eight other offences of theft and dishonesty were taken into consideration. He had committed numerous offences to feed his drug habit and clearly had been out of control in the community.

3.7. At the end of November 1997, he was again released from Young Offender Institution, but his parents became worried about his safety, should he return to reside with them in Derbyshire, as they had apparently received threats from criminals, who were looking for him. They brought him to Westfield and he reported to the Probation Office as being homeless. Initially, his parents had asked his grandmother and other relatives to take him in, but they all declined. His parents then asked Probation and the local authority to house him, but all that could be done was for him to be referred to other agencies. Then apparently by accident, they found someone prepared to house him at an address in Westfield. The situation was far from satisfactory, as the man he resided with, was an alcoholic and refused to let Mr Long let the authorities know the address.

3.8. Mr Long made a good start to the supervision, when he reported well and appeared motived to make a fresh start in Westfield, without getting involved in crime. He made a fresh attempt to remain abstinent of illegal drugs and received support from Probation to do this. Within a few days, he started to go for job interviews and fourteen days later successfully applied to work as an apprentice, in a local engineering works. He was initially well liked by his employers, who described him as being enthusiastic about his job. However, he remained unhappy about his lodgings, which were only on a temporary basis and he spent time looking for alternatives. He was also leading an isolated existence way from his family back in Derbyshire who only managed to visit him on a very occasional basis.

3.9. In January 1998, Mr Long's landlord became concerned that he may be found out to be illegally charging rent whilst claiming housing benefit and gave Mr Long notice to quit. His brother came down from Derbyshire, at that time, and they both looked for alternative accommodation together. On the day of the offence, they went to see their grandmother to ask for her help, but she declined to see them. Mr Long took tablets from his landlord's bathroom cabinet and swallowed a quantity of them without knowing what they were. He and his brother then drank some cider whilst they walked on foot to go and see their uncle in Westfield. They never reached their destination as shortly after this the offence occurred.

3.10. Mr Long has been of no fixed abode for the last four months during which time he has sometimes been sleeping rough or staying with friends, he has recently made, at various addresses throughout London. He also has encountered financial difficulties as a result of not receiving any benefit for a 12 - week period due to administrative problems at the local DSS office. Despite these difficulties, Mr Long has kept in good contact with me throughout this period, when he has reported voluntarily above what is normally required. In view of his difficulties, I have let him see me on occasion, without pre-arranged appointments.

3.11. He has found it hard to live in this area with little or no support from his family and at times he has seemed almost despondent. Despite this, I have always found him to be most considerate, scrupulously polite and co-operative during our discussions. He has been very frank about his offending behaviour and his temptations to offend. Work with Mr Leong has focussed on keeping him motivated towards avoiding offending and helping him find positive solutions to his problems. He has also received some limited financial help from the Probation Service, during the 8- week period he was without benefits. He was helped to write letters of complaint to the DSS and to the local M.P concerning the delays over his benefit. He also has been helped to make applications to five or six Housing Associations. Two of these Associations have offered to house him, as soon as a vacancy occurs and he has been on their waiting lists for the past two months. The Christian Action Housing Association advise me that they may be in a position to offer him a place in the near future. This would be in shared accommodation with the support of a key worker.

4 Risk to the public of reoffending

4.1. Mr Long has committed numerous offences in the past and would therefore appear at high risk of reoffending. Nevertheless, from my discussions with him, I gain the impression that there is a relatively low risk of him committing burglaries or any violent offences in future. He seems more likely to use drugs particularly at times he may feel depressed, but his current drug use would appear to be occasional and significantly less than his high usage last year before he received his custodial sentence. He tells me he has remained totally abstinent of taking heroin but has abused crack cocaine on three occasions since his release. Mr Long acknowledges that he is at risk of reoffending, but appears motivated to try to address his offending. To my knowledge he has avoided committing further offences, over the last few months, even when faced with homelessness and problems with his income support.

4.2. I have been impressed by Mr Long's attitude in supervision. He has good social skills and I think he has potential to do well in the sphere of employment. Before he can achieve this, he desperately needs to gain greater stability in his life and I believe it would be beneficial for Probation to continue to try to assist Mr Long regards this. As a result of a partnership with Turning Point', the Probation Service is now able to offer Mr Long specialist drug counselling in addition to what he has already received in supervision. A Drug Testing and Treatment Order would appear particularly appropriate measure for Mr Long. His return to Court for Court reviews of his progress would serve to keep him motivated. Mr Long can also be given educational and employment advice via the Probation Service. In the long term I believe such measures offer the Courts the most realistic prospect of reducing Mr Long's offending.

5 Conclusion

5.1. Mr Long is at serious risk of being sentenced to a custody today. In addition to this he has offended whilst on Young Offender licence and as a result he has put himself at risk of being recalled to custody. However, I would ask the Court not to take such a course of action as it would undoubtably jeopardise the progress he has made and disrupt any prospect of him achieving a measure of stability to his life. Custody would in many respects be less challenging and demanding for him than life in the community and it would also only result in him being put him back in contact with serious offenders.

5.2. I have considered the option of a Community Service Order, but Mr Long is assessed as unsuitable because he is without a stable address. Much useful work could be done on Probation, but as with Community Service, I must express reservations about the practicalities of supervising a person who is of no fixed abode on Probation.

5.3. In this case, I propose that Mr Long's sentence be deferred for a 3- month period. Mr Long expects to be sentenced to a custodial sentence today and I believe that a deferred sentence would encourage him to stay out of further trouble and encourage him to maintain the progress he has made. Hopefully within three months, he would have gained sufficient stability in his life to enable the imposition of a Community Sentence. Should he successfully complete the deferred sentence period, I would respectfully be suggesting a Drug Treatment and Testing Order as being appropriate in this case.

John Ebrington
Probation Officer

Section 13

The Younger People Start Offending, the More Persistent They Become

Commentary on Court Report 5

The younger the person started offending the higher the risk of them reoffending.
There is an old rule of thumb amongst Probation Officers that the younger an offender started offending the higher the risk of them reoffending. In this case, the offender began offending aged only 12 and soon went on to commit huge numbers of crimes.

Children who truant at high risk of becoming offenders
Children who truant from school are also at high risk of reoffending. It's vitally important that children's transition from Primary School to Secondary School goes smoothly in life. Those children, who for whatever reason, drop out at this stage and start truanting are at very high risk of becoming outcasts from mainstream society and to becoming offenders. Children who drop

out of school at any stage in their school careers are really at significant risk of becoming offenders.

Unacceptable failure to follow up upon absences
It seems really disappointing that no-one followed up upon young Simon Long's absences from school. It would appear that no-one from the school or the authorities took any action in this case for quite a considerable time.

What is going on, why are seemingly more children opting out of going to school?
My impression is that since the pandemic increasing numbers of school children have disappeared off the school register and have stopped going to school. Also, I get the impression that increasing numbers of parents have become dissatisfied with schools and have opted for home tuition, instead of sending their children to school. In a number of cases, this seems to be because they feel schools don't cater particularly well for children with problems and difficulties. One parent even suggested to me that the schools are quite happy for the occasional awkward and academically poor performing child to slip off the register, as their main concern is achieving a good percentage of positive exam results instead. Another concern are the numbers of children being permanently excluded from school. In my home area numbers of exclusions went up by 69% over the past year. This is worrying as those who are excluded would appear at high risk of getting into trouble with the law.

Is it possible for a young offender who dropped out school aged 14 to later turnaround their lives?

In short yes. I recall supervising an offender who was aged 23 years old who had dropped out of school aged 14 years old. He had also committed numerous offences by the age of 23 years old. He seemed bright, articulate and had returned home to live with his Mum, which had restored much needed stability to his life.

He was well-known to the local Police and was constantly being stopped by them. He was a bit of a thorn in their sides, as he was exceptionally well versed in knowing his rights and what the Police are allowed, or not allowed to do. He used to tell me all about it, when he used to come and see me. He seemed to know all about criminal law. He was really amazing.

One day he came in and I flippantly said to him, that he should do a law degree and to my surprise he said he would love to do that. Well, we looked into it. I got him to join the local library and get some books out. He signed up to do a university access course, at the local college in social sciences.

I was really proud of him and told him to bring in his first homework assignment, so that I could help him. He came in and showed me a completed essay. I read it and was flabbergasted, as it was excellent and better than what I could write. I asked him if someone had written it for him, or had he got it from a book and he assured me that he had really written it himself. I told him that it was so good, that he didn't need my help.

Needless to say, he did really well on the course and then successfully applied to do a law degree course at university. I was immensely proud of him, as were the firm of solicitors who had represented him for many years. They offered him work experience, shadowing them working at the local magistrates' court. However, the police objected to him being there and the solicitors had to stop taking him with them to court. Practicing law was going to be very difficult too, for someone such as him with a criminal record. Sadly, I don't think he ever managed to fully complete the degree course, but at least we never saw him as an offender in the Courts again.

Sentencing Simon Long

What did Simon Long look like?
Simon looked bright and friendly. He seemed eager to please and quite intelligent. Although he was sometimes sleeping rough, he always looked clean and tidy.

Simon Long's crime rate rocketed when he became addicted to drugs
Simon Long's offending greatly increased when he was offending to fund his substance misuse. He built up substantial drug debts to those who had supplied him

and had in a big way let them down too. Because of this, he had to quickly move away from Derbyshire.

People in the illegal drug world can be exceptionally nasty and ruthless. I recall that one of my offenders on my caseload had broken ankles. He told me that he had broken them, when he had got drunk one night and had fallen off the balcony at his home. However, I'm given to understand that what actually happened, was that some criminals involved in illegally suppling drugs had got annoyed with him for encroaching upon their area. They paid him a visit and dangled him over the side of the balcony before eventually letting go.

The amount of crime that is drug related in the UK is immense. Tackling Britain's substance misuse problem would undoubtably radically reduce numbers of crimes committed in the UK.

> **How high is the risk of Mr Long reoffending?**
>
> Very low / low / medium / high / very high?
>
> **What risk of harm does Mr Long pose the public?**
>
> Very low / low / medium / high / very high?
>
> **How would you sentence Mr Long?**
>
> **What steps would you take towards reducing the level of youth crime in the UK?**

What steps would you take to improve children's transition from Primary to Secondary Schools?

How would you go about reducing the numbers of children dropping out of attending Secondary School?

What steps would you take towards reducing illegal drug use and substance misuse in the UK?

Section 14

Complete Denial of Any Responsibility for Serious Offences

Report 6

Brief Outline of case:

Court Report 6 has been prepared for Crown Court.
The defendant is David Parry who is aged 20 years. His offences are Burglary, False Imprisonment and Robbery. David Parry claimed he was not guilty and that he had no recollection of committing these serious offences. Concerns are expressed that could he be a psychopath, who will go on to more serious offending?

Commentary on report 6.
The importance of consulting with colleagues and gathering of all other information in preparing court reports is explained.

Instructions:
Imagine you are about to sentence Mr Parry.

Carefully read through the following report. It is based upon a real person and real events that actually

happened. All of the names of people and places have been changed as have some of the details of the defendant so as to protect their identity.

As you carefully read through the report, think about the facts of the case and what happened. Think about the risk posed to potential victims and to the defendant. Also carefully consider the defendant's behaviour and attitudes and their background.

Once you have read the report proceed onto the Commentary on Report 6 section and answer all of the questions before sentencing Mr Parry.

Please also give consideration as to what steps society could take towards reducing similar offences happening in future.

SECTION 14

THE PROBATION SERVICE

This is a pre-sentence report as defined in Section 3(5) of the Criminal Justice Act 1991, it has been prepared in accordance with the National Standard for pre-sentence reports. It is a confidential document prepared specifically for this court hearing.

HARPERBURY Crown Court

Date of Hearing: 30.09. 2000

Full name: David PARRY
Address: 46, Camper Road Ruttlesford

Date of Birth: 03/03/1980
Age: 20 years

Offence and date:
Burglary Dwelling 26/04/2000
Kidnapping/ False Imprisonment 26/04/2000
Robbery: 26/04/2000

Petty sessions area: Ruttlesford

Supervising court: Ruttlesford

Completion date: 27/09/2000

Report Produced by: Mr John Ebrington
official title: Probation Officer

Address:
Probation Office, Civic Centre Ruttlesford Home County. RU23 8P

1 Introduction

1.1. To prepare this report I have seen the papers from the Crown Prosecution Service and a list of previous convictions. I held an interview with the defendant at HMP Bury. I have reviewed Probation Service records about previous periods of supervision and held discussions with the supervising officers, Sally Link, Albert Ford and Jack Waist. I have conducted a standard screening for basic literacy and numeracy skills. I have seen a Pre-sentence report prepared by Sue Naitland for Nattle Magistrates Court on 10/05/99

2 Offence analysis

2.1. Only a custodial sentence would appear appropriate in this case given the seriousness of the offences. Following trial, the defendant was found guilty of all matters by unanimous verdict. The Court has indicated that these were grave offences and that it is considering a lengthy custodial sentence.

2.2. The Court will be aware of the facts of this case following trial. Mr Parry and his co-defendant broke into the victim's home and stole a number of watches, jewellery, two mobile phones, toiletries, sunglasses, cash and a sports bag and its contents. The watches that were stolen were valuable. The victim estimates their total value to be in the region of £12,000.

2.3. The victim returned home shortly before midnight and noticed that one of the windows at the front of the house had been broken. On entering the house, he met one of the two co- defendants in the hallway. The victim was made to go into the kitchen. The defendant then threatened the victim with a long kitchen knife, he had taken from the drawer. The knife was placed with the point of the blade touching the victim's face near to his eye. The defendant threatened to remove the victim's eye. The victim's wallet was taken and he was subjected to threats to divulge his PIN numbers. The victim was unable to recall them. The victim's car keys were taken from him and the perpetrators drove off in his car. On leaving, the telephone wires were cut by one of them.

2.4. The whole incident must have been a dreadful and terrifying ordeal for the victim. In his statement, he said he felt very threatened and intimidated and had no option but to hand over the items that were robbed from him.

2.5. The defendant maintains that he has no recollection of the incident. When I asked him about the victim, he told me he felt unable to express remorse for the victim, because he said that he had no recollection of the incident. Mr Parry spoke of the incident in the third person, as if he were not involved. However, when I challenged him on this and pointed out that he had been found guilty, and discussed the evidence against him, he told me that he believed that he probably was there, but had no recollection whatsoever of taking part.

2.6. Mr Parry maintains that he regularly experiences blackouts and claims that it is a family condition. When asked to explain, he told me that he does things without realising and sometimes ends up in places without realising how he got there. He said that he could not have behaved in such a manner, in committing the current offences, unless he had been experiencing a blackout. He told me that he had been assessed by psychiatrists and by psychologists, who he said, had advised him that these blackouts occur when he gets angry or upset over past events concerning his childhood, when he said he was abused.

2.7. The defendant's account, unless there is medical evidence to support it, appears scarcely credible. In my opinion, he is not facing up to his offence or taking responsibility for his actions. l put it to him, that his attitude towards his offence, at the time of sentence, would have an impact upon the length of sentence that he is likely to serve. However, he told me that he did not care what happened to him. I similarly put it to him, that his attitude and future conduct whilst serving a custodial sentence could have an impact upon his eventual release date. He told me that he did not care, as he felt that there was nothing there for him "in the outside world out of prison."

2.8. During my interview with the defendant, I gained the impression that he is an immature individual, who has poor life skills and a tendency to be egocentric. Probation records suggest that he is a person who is susceptible to being easily led into offending by others. I gain the impression that his co-defendant organised the Burglary offence, and that the defendant chose to go along with him. However, it is certain, that Mr Parry was clearly the instigator of the Robbery Offence, when he displayed nasty violence and menace. I asked Mr Parry if he committed the offence under the influence of alcohol, or drugs and he told me that he did not. He said, that he does not drink alcohol, but regularly abused illegal substances, such as heroin, which he had used about a week before the offence.

2.9. I attempted to discuss the seriousness of the offences with the defendant, but was left with concerns that he seemed to have a poor appreciation of the gravity of what he had done and of the victim's perspective. This appears to be linked to his denial that he has any recollection of being there.

3   Offender Assessment

3.1. The defendant has four previous convictions. His most recent conviction relates to offences committed in April 1999, whilst he was still subject to Young Offender Licence. On this occasion, he admitted to Interfering with a Motor Vehicle and to Taking a Vehicle Without Consent. The offences were committed with another offender and Mr Parry asked for ten other similar cases to be taken into consideration. This to me, seems a worrying spate of offences committed over a short period of time.

3.2. He told the Probation Officer preparing the pre-sentence report that he could recall little about the Taking a Vehicle Without Consent offence because he was heavily intoxicated with alcohol at the time. Whilst he appeared to accept responsibility for his offences, the report author, Sue Naitland, expressed concern over the repetitive nature of his offending, whilst on licence and his apparent lack of regard for victims.

3.3. In 1998, he was convicted of Robbery. This offence has worrying and disturbing parallels with the current Robbery Offence. According to the pre-sentence report prepared for the hearing, the defendant committed the offence against his grandmother. It states that he put his hand over her mouth, ordered her to hand over her purse and threatened to get violent by using a screwdriver he had in his hand. He told the report writer that his motivation for the offence was to obtain money to repay a drug debt, accrued as a result of his addiction to heroin. Such violent and abusive behaviour towards a grand-parent is extremely concerning in my view.

3.4. His earlier conviction in 1998, was for offences of Criminal Damage. One of these involved him entering in an unoccupied dwelling and whilst residing there for several days he caused damage by tearing wallpaper and writing obscenities and other graffiti on the walls. In my opinion, this behaviour appears to have been disturbed and leads me to have further concerns about him.

3.5. His convictions in 1997 concern him being involved with others in Taking Vehicles Without Owners Consent. The theft matter related to clothing being stolen from one of the vehicles. Mr Parry described having experienced a problematic and abusive background which he stated involved neglect by his mother and physical abuse by his stepfather. He told me that they were addicted to drugs. Records reflect that Mr Parry regularly ran away from home at an early age, was also sleeping rough and not attending school. His offending began during this period when he was aged only 11 years.

3.6. It took some time before he apparently came to the attention of Social Services in 1996, when with the assistance of Social Services, he successfully made an application to the Scratching Family Court to be granted a Residence Order to reside with his grandparents. For a six- month period, he attended a special school in Ruttlesford, for children with learning disabilities, where it appears he progressed quite well. Although he left, with no formal qualifications, a recent test administered by the Service reveals that he has no literacy or numeracy problems.

3.7. On leaving school, he went to Ruttlesford College where he gained an NVQ in Catering, but was subsequently dismissed from the course. This he told me coincided with him developing an addiction to heroin and in him leaving his grandparents address. He told me that for a short period he attended for drug treatment at Balance House Drug Rehabilitation Centre in Ruttlesford, but that this was unsuccessful in dealing with his addiction. Mrs Japp manager of Balance house said that in her opinion, it was impressive that he had applied to go there of his own volition, but she stated that once there his behaviour had been rather manipulative and difficult. He refused to attend the therapeutic groups, and became very aggressive to staff, and to some of the other residents, resulting in him being eventually asked to leave.

3.8. Mr Parry has tended to lead an unsettled existence. Following his release from Young Offender Institution in 1999, he resided at the Redland Probation Hostel. However, he was expelled from the hostel for his failure to abide by the evening curfew time, having been previously been warned for such behaviour. For a short period, he returned to live with his grandmother in Ruttlesford, but apparently following disagreements moved to reside in Buryfield. This was also possibly a good thing, as there were concerns over his grandmother's safety.

3.9. Mr Parry moved back to this area, following the imposition of the Community Rehabilitation Order in May 1999. Although he reported as instructed, he immediately expressed concerns about his ability to undertake the Think First programme. He said that he had a history of behavioural problems and anger management problems, and repeatedly expressed doubts about his ability to perform in the group, without losing his temper and creating tantrums.

3.10. The supervising officer, Albert Ford spoke to his grandmother who corroborated this to some extent, and said that Mr Parry had earlier undergone some form of psychological assessment. Interestingly, the records confirm that Mr Parry also told his supervising officer that he experienced blackouts. Mr Parry described these as periods when his anger became so intense, that people who know him, fear for their safety and that following such incidents, he had no recollection of what happened. Mr Ford contacted Social Services and Mr Parry's GP, however there was no response about the possible existence of a diagnosis, or of there being a psychological report in existence.

3.11. Given Mr Parry's reluctance to complete the Think First offending behaviour groupwork condition, the issue was returned to Ruttlesford

Magistrates Court for the local bench to consider. The bench decided to remove the condition and it was agreed that he should undertake the work on an individual basis. Records reveal that some good work was done in trying to address anger management issues with Mr Parry. During the currency of the Order, he also renewed contact with his natural father and this was seen as an encouraging development, as it was hoped that he might be able to exert a positive influence upon Mr Parry.

3.12. The Marlow Probation Office supervised the later stages of the Order. Whilst Mr Parry continued to report as instructed, his supervising officer, Sally Link noted that although he appeared to have been working hard on his offending behaviour, she still considered him at high risk of reoffending. She said that towards the end of the Order, she expressed concerns that he became difficult to engage, reluctant to discuss issues, and noted that he had apparently often been verbally aggressive with the receptionist staff.

3.13. Mr Parry appears to have resigned himself to a custodial sentence. He told me that his family had not been in contact with him since his remand in custody. He told me that his father had advised him that he would "disown" him if he were found guilty and he expressed disappointment over this.

4 Assessment of the Risk of Harm to the Public and Likelihood of Reoffending

4.1. I have very grave concerns about Mr Parry, and I think it that a psychological assessment would be helpful in gaining further insight into his attitudes and his offending behaviour. A psychological assessment could also, in my opinion, assist in making an informed assessment of the risk of him reoffending and harming the public and thus possibly offer some guidance in trying to reduce the risk of him reoffending.

4.2. Probation Officer, Sue Naitland, in her report for Nattle Magistrates Court in 1999, said that, " it is my view that Mr Parry is at relatively high risk of reoffending, his susceptibility to influence, his immaturity, poor problem- solving skills, impulsivity, low level of insight regarding victim issues, together with a lack of lifestyle stability, all contributing in this respect. Mr Parry's risk of harm to the general public appears to be correlated to his use of drugs." I would endorse Sue Naitland's assessment and would add concern in the way that Mr Parry's offending behaviour has escalated.

4.3. In my opinion, the violent offending that appears on his record, is not the result of an anger management problem. During both Robberies, he used violence in a pre-planned and menacing way to get his own way. I suspect that he may be a manipulative individual and that his reported memory losses may amount to nothing more than an unsophisticated attempt to try to distance himself from his offences. Such a stance, together with his lack of victim empathy and the violent and controlling manner of his robbery offences would seem to suggest that he is, in my view, at high risk of reoffending and of causing harm to the public.

4.4. Given that a custodial sentence is inevitable in this case, I would urge that Mr Parry make positive use of his time in custody in terms of trying to reduce the risk of him reoffending. He could usefully reflect upon his offences and carefully consider the victims' perspectives of his crimes. He is strongly advised to learn new employment skills and to participate fully in the offending behaviour programmes that are run by the prisons.

5 Conclusion

5.1. These offences are so serious that only a custodial sentence would appear appropriate. Mr Parry's attitude and behaviour are of grave concern and in the circumstances the Court may consider it appropriate to adjourn for a psychological report in order to shed more light on his concerning behaviour.

John Ebrington
Probation Officer

Section 15

Teamwork is Key in Working with Offenders

Commentary on Court Report 6

A good court report depends upon good communication with others and information exchange.

If this court report had only been based upon purely my interview with Mr Parry, there would have been very little to write about. One of the key ingredients to the report is having sight of the CPS papers. This will include the prosecution's summary of facts, witness statements, including victim impact statements and the defendant's record of previous convictions.

In the 1990's the CPS papers were not always available and previous convictions were often inaccurate

It was important to study these documents before we interviewed the offender. You needed them so that you had a balanced view of the offence and the victim's perspective. On occasion you had to challenge defendant's minimisations and distortions of the truth. However, from my notes I can see that in about 10% of all of the cases I dealt with in the 1990's I never received these vital papers. Even more concerning, I noticed that back in the 1990's some of the offenders record of previous convictions were incorrect as they had some convictions missing. Hopefully this is no longer the case.

Consultation and information sharing
In this case, I consulted widely with probation officer colleagues who gave me interesting contributions which I included in the report, which I feel made it more informative.

Probation officers often initially write these reports in isolation. However, often it is a team effort. I recall I often used to consult with colleagues over various paragraphs in the report. From my notes, I can even spot various sentences and expressions that were the contribution of a colleague.

Once completed the report would always be quality control checked by a colleague.

It seems a shame to me that there seems to be no formal way for Probation to receive information about the offenders from schools, social services and the NHS in the preparation of Court reports. The Probation Service did make enquiries about Mr Parry's possible psychological / mental health issues with his doctors' surgery only to receive no response to their enquiries.

Closer relationships and sharing of information between agencies about people who pose a risk to the public, is important, in order to develop an accurate picture of what is going on. Sharing information about risk posed by individuals, between police, probation, social services, schools and the NHS does help protect the public.

A consultant psychiatrist can make an assessment of a person based upon just one interview. However, if the psychiatrist is advised of the person's behaviour in the community by other agencies, such as probation and others, the psychiatrist will be able to make a better-informed assessment.

Sadly, in my experience, public services under pressure with limited resources are less able to work together well and less able to offer support to people. There can be a growth in waiting lists and some people, with apparent mental health issues, as you will see in Court Reports 7 and 8, can have support withdrawn from them. People with mental health issues do need, whenever possible, be diverted away from the criminal justice system, however too many in my opinion are being caught up in it.

Offenders cooperating with their interviewers and fully admitting their offences and those who deny completely.
It's funny, but my anecdotal experience, is that it is not uncommon for young teenager offenders to completely deny their offences. You can almost imagine them adopting this strategy when they are caught misbehaving

at school. The *"It wasn't me miss I wasn't there,"* type approach. However, as they develop through their teenage years into adulthood, they seem to learn that it is much better to admit your offence and to cooperate with the person who is preparing your Court report. What I call the "It's a fair cop guv" approach. The vast majority of adult offenders, in my experience, tend to be straight forward in fully admitting their offences and in being cooperative with their interviewer. The only offenders who occasionally adopted the complete denial approach, tended to be sex offenders in my experience. Mr Parry, appeared to be the only exception to the rule.

It felt like to me, that Mr Parry was possibly still stuck in the young teenager complete denial approach. Considering that he pleaded not guilty to his offences, I wonder what his trial was like and feel sorry for his victim having to attend court.

Sentencing Mr Parry

What did Mr Parry look like?
He was quite big and appeared very confident, perhaps over confident. He used big gestures with his arms and spoke with conviction about every-thing about himself. He seemed to believe in every-thing he was saying even perhaps if he wasn't telling the truth.

What do you think about Mr Parry's Blackouts?

It was for Mr Parry and his defence team to put forward medical evidence about this, but there was none. However, I believe a psychological assessment of him would be helpful with this regard, but also for other reasons. My main concern is that Mr Parry has already committed a large number offences by the age of 20 and a number of these are very worrying indeed. He seems very manipulative and egocentric and dangerous and I am concerned that he may have psychopathic tendencies. He may be a psychopath and this would need to be diagnosed by a medical professional.

What would you think of this Court report if you were Mr Parry?

How high is the risk of Mr Parry reoffending?

Very low / low / medium / high / very high?

What risk of harm does Mr Parry pose the public?

Very low / low / medium / high / very high?

How would you sentence Mr Parry?

What events during Mr Parry's childhood do you think have contributed to him becoming an Offender?

Poor parenting skills and frequent truanting from

school appear to be common factors in people starting to offend at a young age. People who start offending at a young age are often the most challenging to stop offending altogether. It seems vital to address this issue.

How can we in the UK improve our parenting skills as a country?

How can we reduce the number of children truanting from our UK schools?

When offenders such as Mr Parry become addicted to drugs, they seem to become mini crime waves. In reducing crime in the UK, it would appear vital that we address our substance mis-use problem.

How would you go about reducing the number of drug addictions in the UK?

Why is it vital that a Probation Officer get the Prosecution Papers before interviewing the Offender?

Why is information sharing between agencies about the risk to the public individuals pose so important?

Section 16

A Mentally Unwell Person Gets Caught Up in the Criminal Justice System

Report 7

Brief Outline of case:

Court Report 7 has been prepared for Magistrates Court.
The defendant is Gary South aged 49 years. His offences are Threatening Behaviour and Possession of an Offensive Weapon.

Gary South has been seriously mentally unwell. He behaved in a very bizarre manner and appeared in Court.

Commentary on report 7 debates should not people with mental health problems go to hospital instead of being put through the Criminal Justice system?

Instructions:

Imagine you are about to sentence Mr South.

Carefully read through the following report. It is based upon a real person and real events that actually happened. All of the names of people and places have been changed, as have some of the details of the defendant so as to protect their identity.

As you carefully read through the report, think about the facts of the case and what happened. Think about the risk posed to potential victims and to the defendant. Also carefully consider the defendant's behaviour and attitudes and their background.

Once you have read the report proceed onto the Commentary on Report 7 section and answer all of the questions before sentencing Mr South.

Please also give consideration as to what steps society could take towards reducing similar offences happening in future.

THE PROBATION SERVICE

This is a pre-sentence report as defined in Section 3(5) of the Criminal Justice Act 1991, it has been prepared in accordance with the National Standard for pre-sentence reports. It is a confidential document prepared specifically for this court hearing.

HARPERBURY Magistrates Court

Date of Hearing: 3.11. 1993

Full name: Gary Robert South
Address: 26, Rosewood Road Ruttlesford

Date of Birth: 08.03.1944
age: 49 years

Offence:
Threatening Behaviour and Possession of Offensive Weapon

Petty sessions area: Ruttlesford

Supervising court: Ruttlesford

Completion date: 1.11.1993

Report Produced by: Mr John Ebrington
Official title: Probation Officer

Address:
Probation Office, Civic Centre Ruttlesford Home County. RU23 8P

1   Introduction

1.1. This report is based upon two interviews with Mr. South. I have read the Crown Prosecution Service papers which include a witness statement and Mr. South's record of previous convictions. In addition, I have also consulted Mr. H. Cowen who is the Mental Health Hostel Manager where Mr. South currently resides; Mr. South's Social Worker, Mr. A. Kan, and Ms. T. Markel, a Court Welfare Officer, who has recently prepared a report concerning the South family for the County Court. A medical report has also been prepared for this hearing by Dr. Cowman of Harperbury Psychiatric Hospital which I have seen.

2   Offence

2.1. Given this offence occurred in a chemist shop which was a busy public place, involving innocent bystanders and in particular a young child, it is of serious concern. Mr. South's behaviour, although apparently threatening, could also be described as being irrational. The only contact he had with the four-year old boy was to ruffle his hair. On several occasions Mr. South got to his knees and made the sign of the crucifix. At one time he had a knife resting on his thighs whilst being very close to the child. The child moved off and Mr. South was then seen to put the knife away and whilst doing so, he was said to be muttering gibberish. This behaviour was understandably disturbing for the mother and child.

2.2. When I discussed the case with Mr. South he was visibly distressed by his actions, in particular because there was a child involved. He told me he loves children. Mr South said he had no intention of threatening the mother and child. He said that it was his intention to help and that he was praying to God for the child to get well soon. The purpose of the knife was, he said, for it to be used as a crucifix. Mr South informed me that it was one of a collection of ornamental knives displayed on a wall at his former address which have now been disposed of. About half an hour before the incident there are reports of Mr. South getting on his knees and apparently praying in the Council Housing Department waiting room.

2.3. Following the break-up of his marriage last year, Mr. South made several applications during 1993 to gain access to his children via the County Court. Mr. Smith told me that at the time of the offence in June 1993, he was becoming increasingly frustrated and depressed about not having seen his two children aged 6 and 10 since October last year. It is conceivable that Mr. South's apparent inability to cope with the situation prompted this episode of illness. Dr. Cowman confirms in his report that Mr South was mentally unwell at the time of the offence.

2.4. On 6 June 1993, a day before the incident, Ms. T. Markel, Court Welfare Officer, arranged a meeting for Mr. and Mrs. South and their children at her office. In the event Mrs. South and the children did not attend. When Mr. South attended the Court Welfare office his behaviour at the time led Ms. Markel to have concerns about his mental stability. He apparently behaved in a strange manner in the waiting room and during the meeting with Ms. Markel, he said a number of irrational things.

2.5. Following Mr. South's arrest he was detained overnight and produced at Court the next day. Upon learning this, Ms. Markel contacted the Probation Service at the Court. This intervention and the circumstances surrounding Mr. South's arrest prompted a referral to be made to the Court Mental Health Divisionary Team. Mr. South was then assessed by the Team Leader, Dr Bart, as suffering from "paranoia". Consequently Mr. South was admitted to Harperbury Hospital under Section 2 of the Mental Health Act. Dr Cowman's Medical Report is available to the Court and refers to this.

3 Relevant Information

3.1. Several days before the offence Mr. South received two cautions. One was for possession of an offensive weapon and the other was for the theft of petrol. I believe Mr. South committed these offences whilst being in a disturbed state of mind.

3.2. Mr. South does have a record of committing assaults and offences such as criminal damage. However, it is twelve years since Mr. South was last before the Courts for any offences.

3.3. Interestingly, it was about 12 years ago that Mr. South was first diagnosed as having a mental health problem. Since then, he has experienced a number of episodes of mental illness for which he has received treatment. These seem to coincide with various crises in Mr. South's life. The first diagnosis in 1981, was upon the break-up of his first marriage. Then, following a car crash in June 1988, Mr. South was diagnosed as having a psychotic episode for which he received treatment at Harperbury Hospital. Following the death of his brother, Mr. South was admitted to St. Anthony's Hospital in February 1992 after being disruptive in a local shop. He was discharged in March 1992 and treated as an out-patient until August of that year.

3.4. Mr. South is currently receiving a high level of support. He attends Harperbury Hospital most days of the week and has a Social Worker to monitor his progress in the community. He has been residing at the Mental Health Hostel since September where he receives respite care and supervision from a Key Worker. Mr. H. Bowen, the Hostel Manager, informs me that Mr. South is a model resident and is making very good progress.

4 Risk to the Public of Reoffending

4.1. Mr. South is at risk of developing mental illness when faced with emotional crises in his life. Continued support and treatment for his mental health issues will in my opinion reduce the risk of him reoffending. From my perspective, it is desirable to divert people with mental illness away from the Criminal Justice system and to focus upon helping them get better. Helping Mr. South address the triggers to his mental health illness episodes will assist him also reduce the risk of him reoffending. Coming into contact with other offenders within the Criminal Justice system could raise the risk of him reoffending in my opinion.

5 Conclusion

5.1. Mr. South maintains he had no intention to harm any-one or to be threatening. It was his intention to help. He fully accepts the evidence against him and is ashamed that he was involved in such an incident. Clearly, he was mentally unbalanced at the time and this must have affected his actions.

5.2. Mr. South is prone to mental illness when faced with problems and crises. It is possible that he will behave in a disturbing manner again in the future. Although it is difficult to assess the risk of him actually harming anyone, he has not offended in this way for over twelve years. Previously Mr. South received psychiatric support following his crises. However, now that he has been placed on the Hospital Register by Dr Cowman, he will now receive supervision and support to assist him deal with problems and crises more effectively as and when they arise.

5.3. In the light of Mr. South's mental health problems and the high level of support available to him, I would propose the Court impose a Conditional Discharge. I have considered the possibility of a Probation Order but in view of the psychiatric services he is now receiving together with the strict requirements of a Probation Order, I do not consider any community sentence appropriate. It is also questionable whether Mr South could give informed consent to such an order.

John Ebrington
Probation Officer

Section 17

Mentally Ill People Need to be Better Cared for

Commentary on Court Report 7

Reports number 7 and number 8 are linked as they involve the same offender.

As you read reports numbers 7 and 8, I would like to give you a gentle reminder that although the reports are works of fiction, they are based upon true events that actually happened in the 1990's and that they have all been anonymised, as all of the dates, places and names have all been changed as well as some of the factual details.

Some of the real events that followed Court Report 8 are scarcely believable.

The events that unfold over Court report 8 are scarcely believable in my view. However, they will give you a real insight into things that can happen and can go wrong.

The Police do have powers to take people Psychiatric Hospitals if they appear mentally unwell, instead of charging them with a criminal offence.

It must have been apparent to the Police that Mr South was mentally unwell when they stopped him for theft of petrol and possession of a knife. At that stage, they could have taken Mr South immediately to the local psychiatric hospital for care and assessment. They didn't do this and chose instead to charge Mr South with the theft and the possession of a bladed article and then released him having given him two Cautions. A Caution is only given if someone admits their guilt and it acts like a formal written warning given by the Police. It advises you that no further action will be taken against you on this occasion and that you should remain of good behaviour.

However, if the Hospital had immediately admitted Mr South after the theft and possession of a knife offences, I believe that there was every possibility that he would not have committed the Threatening Behaviour Offence in the Shop. Don't you agree?

What is a Court Mental Health Diversion Scheme?
The whole purpose was to divert people with genuine mental health problems out of the Criminal Justice system. The idea was to have people professionally assessed and if they were ill for them to be offered help and support for their mental health problem. Most importantly, their name was then removed from the Court list so that in effect, they no longer had to appear before the magistrates for sentencing. In other words, the psychiatrist had given a verbal report to the Magistrates confirming Mr South's mental health issues and it

was agreed that he should immediately go to hospital instead of sentencing. It was therefore a mistake and inappropriate for Mr South's case to be relisted and for him to have to appear before the Courts again. On the second occasion, Mr South appeared the Magistrates adjourned the case for the Probation Service to assess Mr South and to prepare a Court Report about him. This was again totally inappropriate, as a psychiatrist from the NHS had already conducted an assessment of Mr South and furthermore the NHS knew an awful lot more about Mr South than did Probation.

Probation do tend to act as servants within the Court system and do as they are asked. If the Court requested a report, we never refused and so the report was allocated to me and I just had to get on with it. In those days, I had a very busy schedule with a very demanding case load. It was not uncommon for me to work extra hours in order to fit it all in and not to be paid for it. In other words, I used to do unpaid overtime, just to keep up with the demands of the job.

Sentencing Mr South

What did Mr South look like?
He had dark hair. He looked middle-aged and was often unshaven. He seemed quite short and surly, and at times quite anxious. He always seemed restless and unable to sit still. There was something furtive about him, but on occasion he was quite eager to please.

What would you think of this Court report if you were Mr South?

How high is the risk of Mr South reoffending?

Very low / low / medium / high / very high?

What risk of harm does Mr South pose the public?

Very low / low / medium / high / very high?

How would you sentence Mr South?

What events during Mr South's life do you think have contributed to him becoming an Offender and what things could have helped him not offend?

How well do you feel the NHS is functioning at present?

What do you think happened at Court when Mr South was sentenced …What sentence do you think he was given?
Mr South was sentenced to 12 Months- Probation. Read the next report to see what happened next.

Section 18

Acute Attention Seeking Behaviour
Report 8

Brief Outline of case:

Court Report 8 has been prepared for Crown Court. The defendant is Gary South aged 50 years. His offence is Dangerous Driving in hospital grounds.

Gary South does donuts and handbrake turns in the hospital grounds. Could this be an acute form of attention seeking behaviour?

Commentary on report 8 discusses a number of topics including care in the community, the killing of Jonathan Zito and a culture of passing the buck between agencies in a climate of limited and depleted resources.

Instructions:

Imagine you are about to sentence Mr South.

Carefully read through the following report. It is based upon a real person and real events that actually

happened. All of the names of people and places have been changed as have some of the details of the defendant so as to protect their identity.

As you carefully read through the report, think about the facts of the case and what happened. Think about the risk posed to potential victims and to the defendant. Also carefully consider the defendant's behaviour and attitudes and their background.

Once you have read the report, proceed onto the Commentary on Report 8 section and answer all of the questions before sentencing Mr South.

Please also give consideration as to what steps society could take towards reducing similar offences happening in future.

THE PROBATION SERVICE

This is a pre-sentence report as defined in Section 3(5) of the Criminal Justice Act 1991, it has been prepared in accordance with the National Standard for pre-sentence reports. It is a confidential document prepared specifically for this court hearing.

HARPERBURY Crown Court

Date of Hearing: 3.08. 1994

Full name: Gary Robert South
Address: 26, Rosewood Road Ruttlesford

Date of Birth: 08.03.1944
Age: 50 years

Offence
Dangerous Driving 08/06/1993

Petty sessions area: Ruttlesford

Supervising court: Ruttlesford

Completion date: 1.03.1994

Report Produced by: Mr John Ebrington
Official title: Probation Officer

Address:
Probation Office, Civic Centre Ruttlesford Home County. RU23 8P

1 INTRODUCTION

1.1. I have discussed the facts of the case with Mr South, read Dr Howard's report and the Crown Prosecution Service Papers. This report is based upon my knowledge of Mr South whilst supervising him on Probation, during the course of which I have liaised with a variety of different agencies. In addition, in November 1993, I prepared a report for Harperbury Magistrates Court.

2 THE OFFENCE

2.1. The fact that Mr. South drove dangerously in the grounds of Harperbury Hospital, putting the public at risk whilst also apparently acting in defiance of the Police, is of great concern. Mr. South tells me he is ashamed of his behaviour. He says at the time he was concerned about his mental well-being and was acutely frustrated, as he felt his condition was not being taken seriously.

2.2. Medical reports reveal that Mr. South sought admission to the Psychiatric Unit on 23, 24 and 26 May and 2 June, 1993 immediately before the offence. On each of these occasions Mr. South was not thought to be suffering from mental illness and was refused admission. On the day of the incident the police were called to escort Mr. South from the premises, as he had behaved aggressively on a previous occasion. In the ensuing days, events occurred at the Housing Office, at the Court Welfare Office and at the hostel where Mr. South was residing which suggest he was becoming increasingly unwell. During this time the police also cautioned Mr. South for several minor offences. Matters culminated on 8 June 1993, when there was an incident at a shop resulting in Mr. South being admitted to Harperbury Hospital under Section 2 of the Mental Health Act. He was subsequently diagnosed as being psychotic.

2.3. Following the break-up of his second marriage, Mr. South made several applications during 1993 via the County Court to gain access to his children. These failed and Mr. South tells me that he became increasingly frustrated and upset about not being able to see them. It is conceivable that Mr. South's inability to cope with the situation prompted this episode of illness.

3 RELEVANT INFORMATION

3.1. Mr. South does have a record of committing offences such as common assault and criminal damage, but was not before the Courts between 1980 and November 1993. Interestingly, it was about 12 years ago that Mr. South was first diagnosed as having a mental health problem. In the intervening years he experienced a number of episodes of mental illness usually coinciding with various crises, such as a car crash, the break-up of his first marriage and the death of his brother. He has received short periods of treatment, but appears more prone to illness when faced with such problems.

3.2. The shop incident on 8 June 1993 resulted in Mr. South appearing at Harperbury Magistrates Court on 8 November 1994. At the time of the hearing Mr. South was described as being well and a model resident at the psychiatric hostel, where he was receiving respite care and regular supervision. He also had a Mental Health Social Worker and the support of an Outreach Team to help with the transition to independent living. Arrangements were in place for Mr. South to be placed on the hospital's Register, which would involve regular medical reviews and community psychiatric nursing support. I did not propose the imposition of a Probation Order as there seemed to be a high level of support in place for Mr. South and I had doubts about his ability to comply with the requirements of National Standards, with its emphasis upon offence-based work, discipline and regular reporting. Nevertheless, a 12-month Probation Order was imposed.

3.3. From the outset of the Order, I concentrated my efforts on liaising with the other agencies working with Mr. South. In my meetings with Mr. South, we discussed problems of concern to him and looked at positive ways of dealing with them. Some such as access to his children, have been difficult. It soon became apparent that Mr. South's planned move to a local authority flat was not going smoothly and he became anxious about this. At about the same time Mr. South made a serious allegation concerning one of the residents at the hostel and he told me he became angry when he felt it was not taken seriously. Although I have limited knowledge of mental health issues, I felt at that time, I was witnessing early warning signs of another episode of illness and expressed my concerns to the other agencies.

3.4. During December, every-thing began to deteriorate rapidly. The community support team declined to assist Mr. South any further, when he became argumentative with them. No progress was made in assisting Mr. South install himself in his flat and following a disruptive incident Mr. South was asked to leave the hostel. Mr. South's Social Worker was transferred to another area and Social Services took the decision not to re-allocate the case to another Social Worker. By the end of the year the Probation Service were the only remaining agency still working with Mr South.

3.5. Mr South began to behave very strangely. He reported to Probation dressed in his pyjamas one day, stating bombs had been planted in his bedroom. I took him to the psychiatric unit, who turned him away stating, there was nothing wrong with him. On another occasion, he insisted in trying to clean everything in my office with a tissue, stating he needed to clean any bombs away. As he appeared to be experiencing another psychotic episode, I immediately drove him to the psychiatric unit, where after a six hour wait, he was assessed by a psychiatrist who turned him away, stating there was nothing wrong with him.

3.6. Mr South appeared at Harperbury Magistrates' Court on Boxing-day for a Breach of the Peace at the Hospital following him being turned away again. Probation made arrangements to place Mr. South at a Hostel for the Homeless. Although Mr. South had been allocated a flat it was unfurnished, without amenities and in a poor state of cleanliness and disrepair. The plan was for him to stay at the Homeless Hostel whilst we tried to get his flat ready. Staff at the Hostel expressed concerns that Mr South was mentally unwell and took him to be assessed at the hospital only for him to be turned away again.

3.7. In trying to organise Mr. South's flat, I enlisted the support of one of Mr. South's relatives. We obtained a grant from the Mental Resources Panel. However, these funds were inadequate and I was fortunate to receive assistance from local churches who donated second-hand furniture for the flat. Once ready, we focussed upon helping Mr South make a successful start in his flat.

3.8. In order to prevent a mental health relapse, I felt it important that Mr. South's treatment and care needed be put on a more consistent footing. I called, with the assistance of the hospital staff, a section 117 hearing under the Mental Health Act for the specific purpose of planning and co-ordinating Mr. South's care in the community. To date, several meetings have been held and Mr. South has responded well and is attending the day hospital on a regular basis. However, Social Services have opted not to allocate him a social worker and to continue to deal with Mr. South only in emergencies.

3.9. Circumstances have conspired for me to become Mr. South's key worker. This has on occasion required considerably more input than is normally afforded to people on probation, thus representing a strain in terms of time. Mr. South has on the whole been polite and co-operative with me, and instances of aggressive or argumentative behaviour have been rare. Mr. South seems to manifest bad behaviour at times of stress, when he feels he is losing his self -control and that this seems to act as a means of attracting attention to himself. I am currently working towards assisting Mr. South to behave more appropriately and to become more self-sufficient. I think it would be a mistake for him in the long term, to become overly dependent on the Probation Service.

4 RISK TO THE PUBLIC OF REOFFENDING

4.1. Mr South would appear at high risk of reoffending

when not in receipt of support for his stress and mental health issues. In order to reduce the risk of him reoffending, his mental health assessments, treatment and care need to be put on a more consistent footing. The inconsistencies that he has experienced have been less than helpful. Once he is mentally well again his transfer from the hospital back into the community will need to be better managed next time.

5 CONCLUSION

5.1. This offence was carried out by a man who was aware what he was doing was wrong but was clearly mentally unwell at the time. This was extreme attention seeking behaviour on his part. A contributory factor to Mr. South's relapse in December 1993, was that he had at the time stopped attending the day hospital at the psychiatric unit.

5.2. As Mr. South's current mental state remains significantly abnormal, it seems to make sense that Mr. South should be required to attend Harperbury hospital on a regular basis. I therefore agree with Dr Howard's suggestions and propose that Mr. South be made subject of a twelve- month probation order with a condition to attend the day hospital at the Harperbury Mental Health Unit where he would be under the supervision of the Consultant Psychiatrist, Dr Howard. However, I do think that Probation should be acting in addition to care in the community rather than in the place of it.

John Ebrington
Probation Officer

Section 19

All of the Agencies Turned Their Backs on Him

Commentary on Report 8

Care in the Community
Care in the Community was quite a discussion point in the news in the 1990's. Basically, it involved many huge Victorian psychiatric hospitals being closed down and the patients being placed in the Community. There were lots of these hospitals dotted around the Home Counties and other parts of the UK that were closed down. They often had huge acreages of land, which were sold off by the Government, for considerable sums to property developers to build houses on.

Many of the former patients were placed in Hostels in local town centres. A number had become quite institutionalised and some of those it was unclear why they had been admitted into the hospitals in the first place. Sad to say that some had been admitted into the psychiatric hospital, purely because they had given birth to a child out of wedlock. How shocking is that?

Killing of Jonathan Zito

Twenty-seven-year-old Jonathan Zito was stabbed to death by mentally ill Christopher Clunis on the 17th December 1992 at Finsbury Park Station. Jonathan was a lovely, kind, sensitive man who was on his way by tube to meet family who were flying into Heathrow from Canada. I actually met him socially, on one occasion, a few days before his death.

Christopher Clunis had been a former in-patient in a psychiatric hospital, who had been released back into the community. He was diagnosed as a paranoid schizophrenic and subsequent enquiries expressed concerns about inadequate psychiatric healthcare given to Clunis. Another concern, was that a number of different agencies were having dealings with Mr Clunis and had failed to share information about him, with each other. It was felt that the death could have been averted, if all of the agencies had shared their knowledge and differing concerns about him.

From this, they came up with the idea of setting up multi-agency risk panel meetings, in order to share information and criminal intelligence about someone. The panel was also tasked to come up with strategies of trying to minimise the risk of harm an offender might pose.

What did Mr South look like?

Mr South was a short, stocky man in his 50's. He tended to have a red face with several days' stubble on it. He was surly and agitated and particularly so when unwell.

Mr South is a problem? Who wants him?
Over the years the emphasis of work at Probation has moved away from social work towards more emphasis upon carrying out risk assessments, tackling offending behaviour and risk management. Mr South was a person who needed help with his mental health issues and social work support.

It was alarming how, as soon as he was made subject to Probation, every-one seemed to abandon him. Within a month or so, he no longer had an assigned social worker and the mental health community support team chose to no longer support him. The mental health hostel with keyworker support, chose to no longer support him, and asked him to leave the hostel. Daycare support at the local psychiatric hospital was withdrawn from him and whenever he presented himself at the hospital he was no longer assessed as having a mental health problem.

Mr South was sometimes awkward and unpleasant to deal with. And in a world of diminishing public resources, it felt like Social Services and the NHS were all too keen to pass the worry of managing Mr South to Probation. It felt like, over to you Probation, you're it!

However, Mr South kept having psychotic episodes when his behaviour and what he said continued to be really quite strange and irrational. On one occasion, he appeared to make some sort of shrine out of the magazines and furniture in the council housing department waiting room and got on his knees and began praying. Perhaps he was praying for some sort of divine intervention for someone to actually help him. On another occasion, he spat on his hands with spittle and then started wiping my desk with his hands stating he needed to help me clean my office. He also checked the waist paper basket to see if there was a bomb in it. These were the actions of a man who was clearly unwell and yet the hospital kept saying there was nothing wrong with him. They told me several times they thought he was faking his symptoms when clearly, he wasn't.

Other dealings with Mental Health Services during that era.
I recall a case of a man on probation to me who was taken off the consultant's list of patients purely because he had been rude to the consultant. In releasing the man from his case-load the consultant said that he felt that Probation was the best agency to deal with the man as he had an "untreatable personality disorder."

Over the years, I had quite a fair number of people with "untreatable personality disorders" on my caseload. The "untreatable personality disorder" diagnosis was the NHS's way of declining to engage with these people or to offer them any form of support.

Also, there were people who were dosing themselves with illegal drugs, because they felt mentally unwell. These people had to come off the drugs first before the psychiatrists would look at them. I can understand that stance, but these people needed support and motivation to address their addictions and this was also difficult to arrange too.

I recall supervising one young person with a Personality Disorder. His name was Tony and he was aged 17 years. Normally, the Probation Service only supervise offenders over 18 years old, but Tony had been passed over to the Probation Service because he had a Personality Disorder and thought to be potentially violent.

I always used to give Tony morning appointments which he routinely missed and then always turned up late on a Friday afternoon when the office was about to shut. By Friday afternoon I was tired and shattered and mentally and physically at a low point and I think Tony deliberately chose this time, because he knew this. I recall working in Youth Justice, with under 18 -year- old offenders, when one young man always used to come in at 4pm on Fridays, because he knew that it was the best time of the week, to get some money out of the Social Workers supervising him.

Tony always seemed very wound up and intense, when he came in and talked as if he had a lot to get off his chest. Conversations with him were always one-way traffic with him, as you could barely get a word in. I recall one Friday when he came late and kept talking intensely at me as I ushered him out by the fire escape, as my colleagues had locked the front door and had all gone home leaving me on my own with him.

As well as getting his appointment times wrong with us, he also kept failing to attend Court too. He had been charged with GBH, to which he said he was pleading not guilty, and he kept failing to attend the Court dates. Every-time he failed to attend, the Magistrates would issue a warrant for his arrest. He didn't take kindly to the Police knocking loudly on his door early in the morning and was grizzly and argumentative with them. The next time he failed to attend Court, 6 police officers went to arrest him and they kicked his door in early in the morning. This apparently upset him greatly, and he waved a kitchen knife at them. On the next occasion he failed to attend, three mini busloads of police went to arrest him, all dressed in riot gear.

Then one afternoon he came in to see me and announced that he had again forgotten to attend Court and he asked me if I could do anything about it, as he feared the riot squad coming round for him early in the morning again. I gave him a calendar to put up on his kitchen wall, for him to enter all of his appointments, in the hope that it might help him keep them. I next phoned the police and offered to drive him over in my car, all on my own, so as to save them the trouble and expense of sending the riot squad in the morning.

People often forget that the Probation Service deal with the exact same offenders as do the police. My colleagues and I would normally go and carry out home visits to offenders' homes all on our own, due to limited resources, whilst the Police would always conduct them in pairs on the grounds of safety.

A possible case of Paranoia.

I recall supervising one man on release from Prison who appeared to have mental health problems. He kept calling the police on the telephone stating people kept knocking on his window at night disturbing his sleep. His theory was that his ground floor bedsit used to be occupied by a sex-worker and that her former customers kept knocking at the window. He also complained to the police that people were following him on foot when he went out shopping at the local shopping precinct. He described teams of five or six people following him around in a clandestine manner. The police contacted me on the telephone and asked me to stop him calling them, otherwise they said they would prosecute him for wasting police time.

The man was fearful and he had a slight learning disability. At the time of his arrest for his original offence, he had spoken freely with the police about who his co-defendants were. This resulted in their arrest and upon sentencing they had threatened to take revenge upon him. He spent his whole time in prison frightened that they would get him, but he was fortunate that the Prison Service deliberately sent him to a different Prison from his co-defendants. They also, as an added precaution, gave him special duties that kept him apart from the other prisoners. However, it was clearly apparent that he felt unsafe now that he had served his custodial sentence.

I spoke to him about his job and he explained that he worked as "a Go-fer" for a small building company.

"What is a Go-fer?" I asked.

"Well, the boss tells me to Go-fer some bricks from the building suppliers and so I go off in the van and pick up some bricks and any other building materials he needs from the suppliers," he told me.

"How is it going?" I asked.

"It's okay, except I got told off by the boss for taking far too long driving to and from the suppliers," he told me.

"Why was it taking so long?" I asked.

"Oh, because I have all of these people in cars following me around and I do detours to try to shake them off from following me. I end up taking twice the time it normally does to do the journey and it's annoying the boss."

He was becoming so anxious that I noticed that he was rapidly losing weight. He also seemed to be possibly becoming paranoid. It was just not feasible to have so many cars following him.

There was no direct link between Probation and the Psychiatric Services and so I encouraged him to book an appointment to see his GP and I sent the GP a short letter outlining my concerns.

Sentencing Mr South

> **What would you think of this Court report if you were Mr South?**
>
> **How high is the risk of Mr South reoffending?**
>
> Very low / low / medium / high / very high?
>
> **What risk of harm does Mr South pose the public?**
>
> Very low / low / medium / high / very high?
>
> **What do you think is the best way of reducing Mr South's offending?**
>
> **How would you sentence Mr South?**
>
> **What events during Mr South's life do you think have contributed to him becoming an Offender and what things could have helped him not offend?**
>
> **In your view are the Mental Health Services the poor relation of the NHS?**

> How well do you feel Social Services are functioning at present?
>
> Do Social Services have sufficient staff and resources in your view?

Section 20

A Post Office Prosecution that Revealed Post Office Incompetence
Report 9

Brief Outline of case:

Court Report 9 has been prepared for Magistrates Court.
The defendant is Melody Larkins aged 62 years and her offence is Theft from Employer.

Melody Larkins' employer, the Post Office paid her a lot of money by mistake and then prosecuted her when she couldn't pay it back, as she had spent it all.

Commentary on report 9 discusses how Melody Larkins' employer the Post Office appear to have been incompetent. Not long after this, one of the UK's largest miscarriages of justice occurred, when numerous sub postmasters were wrongly prosecuted and convicted of crimes they never committed.

I then describe how Ms Larkins became a victim of crime and how the police comprehensively failed to deal with it.

Instructions:
Imagine you are about to sentence Ms Larkins.

Carefully read through the following report. It is based upon a real person and real events that actually happened. All of the names of people and places have been changed as have some of the details of the defendant so as to protect their identity.

As you carefully read through the report, think about the facts of the case and what happened. Think about the risk posed to potential victims and to the defendant. Also carefully consider the defendant's behaviour and attitudes and their background.

Once you have read the report proceed onto the Commentary on Report 9 section and answer all of the questions before sentencing Ms Larkins.

Please also give consideration as to what steps society could take towards reducing similar offences happening in future.

THE PROBATION SERVICE

This is a pre-sentence report as defined in Section 3(5) of the Criminal Justice Act 1991, it has been prepared in accordance with the National Standard for pre-sentence reports. It is a confidential document prepared specifically for this court hearing.

HARPERBURY Magistrates Court

Date of Hearing: 3.08.1994

Full name: Mertle LARKINS
Address: 26, Downtrodden Road   Lower Ruttlesford

Age: 62 years

Offence
Theft from Employer

Petty sessions area: Ruttlesford

Supervising court: Ruttlesford

Completion date: 1.03.1994

Report Produced by: Mr John Ebrington
Official title: Probation Officer

Address:
Probation Office, Civic Centre Ruttlesford Home County. RU23 8P

1 INTRODUCTION

1.1. I have held two office interviews with Ms. Larkins and read the Prosecution papers provided by the Post Office Solicitors and have discussed these with the defendant.

2 OFFENCE ANALYSIS

2.1. Ms. Larkins was mistakenly overpaid by her employers for a period of 15 months between 1996 and 1998 and Ms. Parkins failed to notify them of this error.

2.2. Ms. Larkins says she did not examine her pay slips closely, but was aware that she was being overpaid and that the money was not hers to spend. When Ms. Larkins received her P60 in April 1997, she says she was shocked when she realised by how much she had been overpaid during the year. She says she felt the situation had got out of hand and went through a period of panic- stricken indecision in the month prior to the mistake being found out. The net over-payment during the 15 months amounted to some £8,141.31.

2.3. Ms. Larkins fully accepts she was in the wrong and states she is very ashamed of her actions. She says she spent the bulk of the money on buying items, such as clothes, and shoes for her children and her grandchildren. The Post Office demanded she immediately repay the over-payment, but Ms Larkins states she was unable to do so. Ms Larkins' inability to repay the money resulted in Ms Larkins' prosecution and in her immediate dismissal.

3 RELEVANT INFORMATION ABOUT THE OFFENDER

3.1. Ms Larkins has no previous convictions and according to the Post Office Prosecutor, she has an exemplary work record with the Post Office. Ms. Larkins originally trained and then qualified as a State Registered Nurse. She left in 1969 to bring up her children. However, both Ms. Larkins and the children experienced an unsettled and difficult relationship with her husband. The couple separated a number of times, before eventually divorcing in 1979.

3.2. Following the divorce in 1979, Ms. Larkins went back to work as a Sorter in the Post Office, working shifts, and bringing up her children as a single parent. Although she had some support from her extended family, she did encounter some difficulties and her house was repossessed when she was unable to meet the mortgage repayments, the family eventually being rehoused into Council accommodation.

3.3. After undergoing training, in 1984 Ms. Larkins went to work as a Counter Clerk in a busy Post Office in the West End. Such a post, in my opinion, carries with it a high degree of responsibility and demands proficiency in a multitude of functions carried out by the Post Office. I feel it is much to Ms. Larkins' credit that the Post Office states she was a first- class employee.

3.4. In 1995 Ms. Larkins' hours were reduced and in return she received compensation and an annual pension. She explains there was initially some confusion, as she was at first offered work of 20 hours per week which was reduced to 15½ hours, as any hours above this affected her pension. A year later, in 1996, Ms. Larkins was transferred to another Post Office and it was then that she was mistakenly paid as a full-time employee.

3.5. Ms. Larkins has eight children aged between 18 and 29, and eleven grandchildren. I gain the impression that Ms. Larkins, has over the years dedicated herself to her family, raising her children almost single handed in difficult circumstances and now that they are adults, she still remains supportive of them. It is a credit to Ms. Larkins' efforts, that none of her children have ever been in trouble and are all either actively employed or pursuing educational courses. Ms. Larkins eldest daughter is currently attending a degree course at university and Ms. Larkins assists by looking after her children.

3.6. Ms. Larkins presents as being acutely distressed

and ashamed of her offence. She has recently been diagnosed as a having an over-active thyroid. As a result of this and perhaps also, because of the stress involved in attending Court, Ms. Larkins describes having spent numerous sleepless nights and having lost some three to four stone in weight. Ms. Larkins was dismissed from the Post Office, but is in receipt of a pension of £3,520 per annum. She expresses a wish to repay the money overpaid.

3.7. Ms. Larkins says she is unhappy in the area where she is living and expresses a strong desire to move. She says she would like to return to some form of part-time employment, but has doubts about her prospects. However, as a measure to keep herself active and give herself a fresh start, she is currently undertaking a part-time NVQ Level 1 Course in Floristry.

4 RISK TO THE PUBLIC OF REOFFENDING

4.1. Ms. Larkins has until now led a blameless life and I very much doubt that she will ever come before the Courts again. She presents as being a low risk to the public.

5 CONCLUSION

5.1. This offence was unsophisticated and it seems inevitable that it should have been noticed sooner or later. The fact that it emanated from an error and took so long for the Post Office to rectify the situation, does seem to point to a degree of incompetence on their part. However, as Ms. Larkins did not notify them of their mistake and, in view of the large sums involved, this offence represents a serious breach of trust.

5.2. The Court may be considering a custodial sentence in this case. I would argue against such a sentence. This is Ms. Larkins first occasion before the Courts and in my opinion, she does not pose any future risk to the public. I doubt her ability to cope in the harsh environment of prison and such a sentence would also punish her family.

5.3. In this case I propose a medium- term Combination Order of Probation and Community Service. Although Ms. Larkins does have health problems, she is medically fit to undertake work. Ms. Larkins is assessed as suitable to undertake Unpaid Work on Community Service and I believe she has a number of qualities to contribute towards the scheme. The aims of the Probation element of the Combination Order would be to assist Ms. Larkins make a fresh start, assist her to monitor her income and expenditure, move home if she so wishes and to seek alternative employment.

John Ebrington
Probation Officer

Section 21

Not Only Were the Post Office Incompetent, so Were the Police

Commentary Court Report 9

How do you view the Post Office's role in this case and the way they dealt with it?
Firstly, the Post Office appear incompetent in the way they over paid Ms Larkins and that it took them so long to notice their error.

Secondly, the Post Office's main motive appears to have been to recoup the money overpaid. However, they did not grant Ms Larkins any time to repay the money owed. Most employers agree to gradual repayment of the money, by organising monthly deductions from their pay.

Thirdly, the Post Office only chose to prosecute and dismiss Ms Larkins when she was immediately unable to repay the money. That suggests that possibly in their view she would not have committed an offence if she had repaid the money when asked. This seems illogical as surely their main argument that a breach of trust had occurred still remained.

The Post Office prosecuted this case. They were uniquely her employers, victim and prosecutor in this case. No other organisations have this setup. Do you envisage any problems with it?

The problem with such a set-up is that there are no checks and balances within it. The CPS act as checks and balance for police prosecutions and the CPS prosecute people in a fair and impartial manner.

Are you aware of any other Post Office Prosecutions?

In fact, during this period, one of Britain's most widespread miscarriages of Justice occurred due to the Post Office wrongly prosecuting numerous sub postmasters for Fraud, when in fact the apparent losses at the sub post offices were not losses at all, but computer errors caused by the Post Office's own faulty Horizon Computer system. This huge miscarriage of Justice came to light, when 555 former sub postmasters took legal action against the Post Office.

Those prosecuted were dealt with in a disgraceful and appalling manner by the Post Office. The main aim of the Post Office appears to have been to recoup the apparently fictitious losses thrown up by the Post Office computer system. These were often huge sums of money involving tens of thousands of pounds. Many sub postmasters were forced to take out substantial loans or even sell property in order to re pay these sums created by the faulty computer system. Many people were wrongly sent to jail, causing innocent families deep upset and extreme hardship. Many concerns have also been expressed that the Post Office were grossly unfair and dishonest in the way they conducted themselves.

Many victims were falsely told that they were the only ones to experience these apparent computer problems, when this was blatantly untrue. To make matters worse, it would appear that the Post Office began to realise that they had serious deficiencies with their computer system that was causing problems, but ignored them and actively covered up the problems, whilst continuing to victimise the sub postmasters.

I highly recommend listening to Nick Wallis' podcast, "The Great Post Office Trial" on BBC sounds. Nick Wallis also helped write an article about it in Private Eye which is currently accessible on the internet. He has also written an excellent book, *"The Great Post Office Scandal: The fight to expose a multimillion- pound IT disaster which put innocent people in jail."*

I recall working at my local Crown Court one day and witnessing a woman in her 30's, who was one of these sub-post-office people being sent to jail, and all of her assembled family in Court, looking ashen grey and deeply distressed. I remember one of my Probation Officer colleagues telling me that she felt there was something seriously wrong with these Post Office cases going through the Courts, at that time, that she found very troubling. Well history has shown that her instincts were right.

It is estimated that in the region of 3,500 sub-postmasters were wrongly blamed for Horizon computer losses and that around 700 were wrongly found guilty of crimes. 236 are believed to have been wrongly sent to prison. To date 93 wrongful convictions have been overturned by the Court of Appeal.

Since writing the last few paragraphs, the ITV drama "Bates v Post Office" has been shown on the Television and brought this issue to the general public's attention. Widespread concern and dismay has been expressed about the sub postmasters appalling mis- treatment and how slowly it has taken for people's convictions to be overturned and for people to be paid compensation. Even more victims appear to have come forwards and the issue has been debated in the House of Commons. A number of sub-postmaster victims have been interviewed in the media and their testimonies have been heart-wrenching. The ITV drama has really effectively put over how real people 's lives can be so adversely affected by the Criminal Justice system and particularly when it gets things wrong. The plea-bargaining that went on was grossly unfair. Also access to legal aid was slashed over this period, which made things even more difficult for all of these people wrongly accused.

How Ms Larkins became a victim of crime whilst subject to a Probation Order.

One day Ms Larkins came in for her probation appointment as usual, however she accidentally left her handbag under her seat in the waiting-room, when she came into the interview room with me. Within a few minutes of sitting down in the interview room she realised what she had done and we rushed back into the waiting-room to recover her handbag, but it had gone. Someone had stolen it. Ms Larkins was upset as the handbag contained £100 in her purse, her bank and credit cards and her passport.

The office manager checked the office CCTV and saw and recognised the person who had stolen the handbag. The person who had stolen it was the boyfriend of someone who was on Probation. The theft was reported to the Police and the person's name and address was handed to the Police. Nothing happened. The Police took no action, even though they knew the name and address of the offender and that we had video evidence of the theft.

After a month of inaction, I helped Ms Larkins write a letter of complaint to the police and we later received an apology from them. I don't know what was happening with the police at the time. I don't think that they were particularly lacking in resources, but I think it was more about what work they chose to prioritise. I remember going to Court and getting the Magistrates to issue warrants for the arrest of people who had failed to attend their Breach of Probation hearings at court. However, the Police never seemed to execute these court warrants for their arrest, even though they knew where they lived. In other words, they never went round to arrest people for Breach of Probation. It seemed like they were contemptuous of court warrants issued for Breaches of Probation. Even the local newspaper wrote an article about the police's failure to execute warrants. Were the police lacking in resources or was it more about what were their priorities and poor time management? What do you think?

Sentencing Ms Larkins

What would you think of this Court report if you were Ms Larkins?

How high is the risk of Ms Larkins reoffending?

Very low / low / medium / high / very high?

What risk of harm does Ms Larkins pose the public?

Very low / low / medium / high / very high?

What do you think is the best way of reducing Ms Larkins offending?

How would you sentence Ms Larkins?

What events during Ms Larkins' life do you think have contributed to her becoming an Offender and what things could have helped her not offend?

Section 22

An Unusual Offence of Indecent Behaviour by a Woman

Report 10

Brief Outline of case:

Court Report 10. Magistrates Court.
Eva Damitriu aged 25 years. Begging with a three-year-old child and Indecent Behaviour.

Eva Damitriu indecently exposed her genitals as a way of trying to avoid being arrested for begging. Other passengers on the tube described feeling shocked by her behaviour.

Commentary on report 10.
How would you sentence Ms Damitriu?

There is a discussion about Asylum seekers who might commit an offence and about men who send out women and children to commit offences. What do you do if you see someone you are supervising on Probation offend? There are a few anecdotal stories of the occasions it happened to me.

Instructions:
Imagine you are about to sentence Ms Damitriu.

Carefully read through the following report. It is based upon a real person and real events that actually happened. All of the names of people and places have been changed as have some of the details of the defendant so as to protect their identity.

As you carefully read through the report, think about the facts of the case and what happened. Think about the actions of the victim and the defendant. Also carefully consider the defendant's behaviour and attitudes and their background.

Once you have read the report proceed onto the Commentary on Report 10 section and answer all of the questions before sentencing Ms Damitriu.

Please also give consideration to what steps society could take towards reducing similar offences happening in future.

THE PROBATION SERVICE

This is a pre-sentence report as defined in Section 3(5) of the Criminal Justice Act 1991, it has been prepared in accordance with the National Standard for pre-sentence reports. It is a confidential document prepared specifically for this court hearing.

MAGISTRATES COURT

Date of Hearing: 3.08. 1996

Full name: Eva Damitriu
Address: 26, Downtown Road   Lower Ruttlesford

age: 25 years

Offence
Begging with a child
Indecent Behaviour

petty sessions area: Ruttlesford

supervising court: Ruttlesford

Completion date: 1.08.1996

Report Produced by: Mr John Ebrington
official title: Probation Officer

Address:
Probation Office, Civic Centre Ruttlesford   RU23 8P

1 Introduction

1.1. I have interviewed Ms Damitriu on one occasion at this office with the assistance of interpreter Ms Helena Walkingson, when we discussed the contents of the Crown Prosecution witness statements and her antecedents. Ms Damitru recently appeared at Harley Street Magistrates Court on the 04.06.96 and was sentenced to a two-year Conditional Discharge for an offence of Begging with a child which took place on the 13.04.96. I have had access to the pre-sentence report which was prepared for the Court on that occasion.

2 Offence Analysis

2.1. A plain clothes policeman on patrol on the Piccadilly line observed the defendant begging on a tube carriage. When he boarded the train and showed her his warrant card, she began to shout loudly at him. Whilst he was trying to arrest her, she sat down on the carriage floor and took out her breast and placed her baby on it. Whilst continuing to shout at the policeman, she raised her dress, revealing no underwear, and exposed her genitals. For a short while, she appeared to be refusing to accompany the police officer off the train. Eventually, she did leave the train, as requested, and sat down on a bench on the platform when she then proceeded to hit herself around her face. The police officer described her as being "hysterical" and expressed concern that she made a gesture as if to throw her young baby on the railway line. Ms Damitriu committed this offence whilst she was on police bail to appear at Harley Street Magistrates Court on the 04.06.96, for another offence of begging with a child on the Piccadilly Line.

2.2. Ms Damitriu says that she was begging because she was short of money for clothes and nappies for her baby and for food for her family. When she at first saw the plain clothes police officer, she says that was initially unsure who he was but then realised he was a policeman. She says that she somehow felt more fearful of a plain clothes officer as opposed to one in uniform and says she became very distressed and panicked. She recalls sitting on the floor and protesting, but gives a confused account of her indecent behaviour stating she was in a highly agitated state and did not know what she was doing. She says that she appreciates that the public and the police must have been shocked by her behaviour. She says that she immediately apologised to the police following her arrest. Ms Damitriu says that her husband had not been aware of these offences at first and that when he found out he was very angry, and that her behaviour caused a lot of arguments. She expresses feelings of shame and guilt, and wishes to apologise unreservedly to the Court for her behaviour. She adds that she wishes to promise never to behave in such a way again.

3 Relevant information about the offender

3.1. Ms Damitriu and her family came to this country four months ago. Her husband told me that they were seeking political asylum, due to racial and ethnic hatred in their country. He explained that since the death of their gypsy parliamentary representative their situation in Romania had become very difficult and they hoped to be able to settle and lead a better life in this country.

3.2. Ms Damitriu describes growing up in a small house in a rural part of Romania. She says that she did not go to school, because gypsies were unwelcome there and excluded from mainstream society. She adds that in any event, she would not have been able to afford the school uniform. She says that her parents died within several months of each other when she was about 12 years old, and that she brought up her younger brother with the assistance of other members of her family.

3.3. Ms Damitriu and her family currently resides in a two- bed roomed flat which they share with another couple and their child who are relatives. The family are dependent on state benefits of £160 per fortnight. She says that they are currently unable to seek employment due to their status and that her husband is in any event unable to work due to a medical condition. Ms Damitriu was expecting a baby in March but recently had a miscarriage for which she has been in receipt of some hospital treatment. She tells me that the family receive some limited support from the local social services who give them information and advice.

4 Risk to the public of reoffending

4.1. It is of concern that Ms Damitriu has now received two convictions for begging with a child within a short space of time. As previously stated, on the last occasion she was sentenced to a two- year Conditional Discharge, which she is not in breach of, as this offence took place beforehand. I asked her if she could recall what had happened at Court on the last occasion and she did not seem to remember or understand what a Conditional Discharge is. However, she did seem to recall someone telling her that if she offended again, she might be sent to prison which would result in her being separated from her baby.

4.2. My impression is that Ms Damitriu was well aware that the plain clothes officer was a policeman and that she reacted in the way she did, because she feared being arrested and in her own way tried to avoid being arrested. We spent some time discussing her offences and how other passengers on the tube might have felt about her behaviour and I think she now understands why the Court takes a serious view of such behaviour. However, my impression is that her husband has been telling her to go out begging. Other Romanian Gypsies have recently been arrested and prosecuted for similar offences and they have all been women. It would appear that the pattern has been for the men stay at home whilst their women folk are sent out to beg. I fear that her husband may pressurize her to continue to beg and that as a consequence there might be a fairly high risk of her reoffending unless she is able to assert herself more.

5   Conclusion

5.1. I would ask the court not to impose a custodial sentence today as I feel it would have a negative impact on Ms Damitriu and her family.

5.2. I have discussed with her the possibility of the imposition of a Community Service, Unpaid Work Order. However, as she is still currently breast feeding her baby, this would not appear to be an appropriate option. She is therefore assessed as being unsuitable.

5.3. With regard to Probation, Ms Damitriu expressed her willingness to abide by the requirements of such an Order. However, whilst such a measure could usefully monitor her future behaviour, I do not think that there are many offence- based issues to focus on with her on an Order. Whilst she indicated that she would like a forum to discuss welfare issues, I feel that these issues are currently appropriately being addressed by Social Services.

5.4. The court does have the option of imposing a financial penalty. Having to make payments would serve as a regular reminder of the court's disapproval of her behaviour. However, as her offences were financially motivated the Court could take the view that such a measure might be counter- productive. In this case I propose that Court consider giving her another Conditional Discharge. I have carefully explained the meaning of such a measure and she is aware that this allows the Court to retain fully its sentencing powers for these matters should she come before the Courts again.

John Ebrington
Probation Officer

YOU, THE SENTENCER - WHAT WOULD YOU CHOOSE?

Section 23

When a Probation Officer Witnesses Someone they are Supervising Commit an Offence
Commentary on Court Report 10

Ms Damitriu was sentenced by the Court to 12 Months- Probation!
Well, the interpreter and I used to regularly meet with Ms Damitriu. She was illiterate and had never learnt to read the time on a clock. I think that she was totally in the control of her husband, who told her when to set off from home to walk to the Probation Office for her meetings with us. She used to come along with her three -year -old boy, who she liked to put on to feed from her breast during our meetings. Was this a normal thing for her to do? Or was she deliberately trying to make me feel uncomfortable? Who knows, any way we set about teaching her how to read the time on the clock and how to read and write. It was a bit of an uphill struggle, but we felt it might help her to possibly go in a positive direction in life.

We explored with her legitimate ways of obtaining

money other than begging and constantly reminded her not to reoffend, as she was at risk of being sent to jail next time. Being an asylum- seeker, she was not allowed to work and so we looked at what charity support there was for asylum seekers.

Guess what! Those of you who consider her as being at high risk of reoffending were right, as she did reoffend! But more of this later.

What do you do when you see someone you are supervising offending?

I remember this happened to me, when I first worked for Probation as a Community Service Officer. I was out and about in my car, when I spotted someone driving who shouldn't be, as I knew they had been disqualified. What do you do? Well, I asked my line manager who was a retired Police Officer and he suggested I contacted the Police Criminal Intelligence Unit on the telephone. The advantage of doing this, was that you didn't have to give any witness statements, or get involved in any prosecutions. Basically, you were passing on the information to the police for them to deal with. The other thing was that your identity was kept confidential. Only the Criminal Intelligence Officers knew who you were and they would never pass on who had given them the information to their police colleagues. What I also found, was that the Intelligence Officers were, on the whole, quite straight forward and pleasant to deal with, as compared with normal rank and file officers. Over the years, I built up quite a positive relationship with the

Criminal Intelligence Officers.

The delights of being a Probation Officer on Office duty.

We used to have to take it in turns to be on Office Duty. What it involved was that you used to have to see the service users who had come in to see Probation Officers who were either on holiday or off sick. I recall that computers had now recently arrived on our desks and we were now required to do all of our own typing of letters and Court Reports. It was a massive job and the two fingers that I use for typing have become quite distorted and bent over the years. There was a room full of people, who used to do all of our typing for us, now with not a lot to do, and yet they still always, used to put through all sorts of stupid random phone calls to you, as 'Office Duty,' when I think they could have dealt with them.

I recall one Friday afternoon in between furiously typing a court report and seeing colleagues' service users, I had a phone call put through to me, from someone who was asking for advice, about how do you go about becoming a Probation Officer. I felt like saying honestly, don't bother, as the job is just much too much.

The next two phone calls put through to me to deal with, were people who wanted to talk to me about probate, as they thought that we delt with probate and that is what Probation Officers dealt with. Oh, come on, why were those phone calls put through to me, by those people who used to do all of our typing, who were now just sitting there, reading magazines. Their days were numbered, as they either left or were relocated to tasks involving a lot of hard work.

Finally, the last telephone call of the day was from one of our service users who told me, that he believed that the police had secreted listening devices all over his flat and were passing an electric current through his bed to stop him sleeping at night. He said that he was nevertheless, a superman, with special powers, that he was going to use against the police, who he said he hated, as he was so angry with them. I didn't know what to do with the information at first, but after chatting with colleague, we felt it best to contact the Police Criminal Intelligence Unit. I gave them a call and apologetically said that hoped that I wasn't wasting their time by telling them about the strange phone call.

When I came in, on the following Monday morning, there was a telephone from the local Criminal Intelligence Officer. He thanked me and praised me for giving him that information on Friday afternoon, as he said that, over the weekend, there had been a Police 'call out' to this man's address and apparently, thanks to my phone call, the police said that they knew exactly what they were dealing with. Apparently, he had attempted to fly just like Superman, but sadly his attempt had failed.

Sometimes, giving information to the Criminal Intelligence Officers could have a huge impact.
There was a period during which I used to supervise a

man, who had a record of having committed some very violent offences over the years. I used to have this way of encouraging him to chat away to me in a friendly way. There was a big football match due to take place at the local football stadium, between the two local rival football teams, in several weeks' time and he told me that a fight had been arranged between the two sets of rival football hooligans, on match day outside a specific pub in the town.

Any-way, as soon as he left, I contacted the local Criminal Intelligence Unit on the telephone and told them all about it and that I was particularly concerned given the history of the person who had told me.

I forgot all about that conversation when I went to the football match, as usual, several weeks later. I was a bit taken aback that as I left the stadium after the game, there was a huge Police presence and one of the officers was announcing over a Tannoy, that all of the local pubs had been shut and that we were all to go straight home. It took a while for the penny to drop, but then it came to me, and I remembered my call to the Criminal Intelligence Unit and realised that my actions had mobilised all of these police officers. Wow, the power of a single phone-call!

Who said Ms Damitriu was at high risk of reoffending?
I was travelling on the Piccadilly line Underground train one day. I was standing opposite the exit doors getting

ready to get off the tube at Tottenham Court station. When the train stopped, at the station before Tottenham Court Road, I saw Ms Damitriu get on the train at the far end of the carriage and then start begging. I can only guess, that she had been gradually working her way down the train, by changing carriage when it got to a station. She was definitely begging and was slowly working towards me. "Oh no", I thought to myself and I hoped I would be able to get off at the next station before she saw me. But just as the train was about to stop, at Tottenham Court Station, she proffered her hand towards me and asked me for money. On doing so, I saw that she recognised me and I waggled my finger at her and shook my head in a big and exaggerated way as if to portray huge disappointment and then got off the train.

I repeated the huge head shaking gesture as soon as she came in for her next appointment. Before I said any-thing, she then told me via the interpreter, that it wasn't her that I had seen, as she had a hospital appointment at that time. Even the interpreter seemed quite convinced by her explanation.

"Hang on a minute! I hadn't said any-thing about having seen you begging on the tube yet", I interjected.

The interpreter suddenly nodded in agreement and confirmed that she also had not said any-thing about me seeing her begging either.

"You are lying and only repeating what your good for

nothing husband told you to tell me," I said. "Well, you can tell him that I have advised the police that I have seen you and that they are now going to be watching out for you. Tell him that next time you are going to Prison and he will actually have to do something, for once, as he will be left to look after you child on his own. He had better start learning now, or stop sending you out to beg," I continued.

I don't know if my little rant at her had the desired effect, but I can confirm that she managed to complete her Probation Order without being arrested for any-thing.

Sentencing Ms Damitriu

What did Ms Damitriu look like?

I recall that she had long dark hair, often in pigtails and was quite short in stature. She wore traditional gypsy looking clothing. She spoke in Romanian all of the time. She rarely smiled. Although I couldn't understand what she was saying and always needed an interpreter to assist me. I recall she always sounded like she was complaining all of the time, as she had a rather loud, whining, sounding voice. I'm fairly sure nothing very positive used to come out of it.

What would you think of this Court report if you were Ms Damitriu?

> **How long has Ms Damitriu been in the UK and how many times has she been arrested for Begging during that time?**
>
> **How high is the risk of Ms Damitriu reoffending?**
>
> Very low / low / medium / high / very high?
>
> **What risk of harm does Ms Damitriu pose the public?**
>
> Very low / low / medium / high / very high?
>
> **What do you think is the best way of reducing Ms Damitriu offending?**
>
> **How would you sentence Ms Damitriu?**
>
> **What events during Ms Damitriu's life do you think have contributed to her becoming an Offender and what things could have helped her not offend?**
>
> **How long do you think it was taking to process asylum seekers in the UK at the time of Court Report?**

There was a big back log of asylum seeker cases at that time as there is today. Back in the 1990's, it was taking 18 months to two and a half years to process their claims. I suspect Ms Damitriu and her family were aware of this, and that their claim for asylum was not particularly genuine. I also doubt that they had any long-term desire to remain in the UK any-way.

Ms Damitriu's arrest for begging was not an isolated incident, as quite a lot of Romanian Gipsy women were being arrested for begging at around that time.

The problem became such, that in 2000, arrangements were made to pass people's details to the immigration services when arrested for begging so that decisions regarding their asylum claim application could be fast tracked.

Section 24

Suitability for Parole Report

Report 11

Please read this report and decide if Mr Aylin should be granted Parole or not.

PROBATION SERVICE
16 June 1998

PAROLE ASSESSMENT REPORT

Huseyin- Huseyin Aylin aged 49 years
HMP Castletown.

Proposed release address: 91, Bedstead Avenue
Harperbury.

1 Basis of Information

1.1. I have read through Mr Aylin's Probation records which include details of his offences and previous reports. His case was recently transferred to me in May 1998, however since then I have held two lengthy interviews with him and have had opportunity to meet with members of his family.

2 Proposed release address

2.1. I can confirm that I have verified the proposed release address as being suitable. It is the home of his 72 -year- old mother, who is a woman of independent financial means and who is supportive of her son. She lives in a four bedroomed house in a quiet residential area in Harperbury. Mr Aylin has assisted his mother with practical tasks around the home whilst on leave. He and his mother appear to get on well together and I do not envisage any problems.

3 Family's Attitude towards the Offender

3.1. Mr Aylin and his partner first met in 1976 and they have three children together. There are two daughters aged 19 and 20 years and a son aged 15 years. The eldest daughter had a baby in February this year. Mr Aylin has taken an active interest in his children whilst serving his sentences and has kept in regular contact with them. The children frequently communicate with him and have visited him regularly. They would appear to be very fond of him, but have also made it clear that whilst they have forgiven him, they do not approve of his past offending behaviour in any way. They also feel that they have suffered greatly as a family because of his actions.

3.2. Case notes describe Mr Aylin as having a dominant personality in over seeing his family prior to his imprisonment and reveal that his family encountered difficulties following his sentence in 1987. The family home was repossessed and the family were housed in temporary accommodation for some time before being permanently housed. During this period, records indicate that Mr Aylin's partner appeared to be experiencing some form of depression and seemed to have difficulties in managing day to day affairs. In 1990 it became apparent his son Benol was experiencing behavioural problems at infant's school. This resulted in him being admitted for therapy at Great Ormond Street Hospital and he has since been sent to a special school for children with learning disabilities. To his credit, it was Mr Aylin himself who initially alerted the authorities to the problems his son appeared to be facing. He was granted leave, from

Prison to attend meetings with social services, whilst his son was on the 'At Risk Register' for a short period and records indicate that he played a positive role in those meetings.

3.3. I have not had an opportunity to speak with Mr Aylin's ex-partner, Ms Hayes. From what Mr Aylin tells me, she was furious with him, after his offences and has since had limited contact with him. During his time in custody, she has apparently become a very religious person. What limited contact there has been, Mr Aylin tells me, has been cordial. Mr Aylin has expressed a wish for reconciliation with his ex-partner and to be reunited his family. However, from what he says, indications are that Ms Hayes remains reluctant, but is prepared to have a platonic relationship with him. Apart from the youngest child, the other children are now adults. Mr Aylin expresses praise for the eldest daughter, who he states has responded well and responsibly to his father being in custody and appears to have become comparably a more mature young woman as a result.

4 Work Prospects

4.1. Mr Aylin owns the freehold of a small retail outlet, which is currently run as a restaurant by tenants. He plans to take over the lease after his release and to continue to run the premises as a restaurant.

5 Offender's attitude to his Offences and to victims

5.1. For an offence of importation of 2.9 kg of heroin, Mr Aylin appeared at Middlewell Crown Court on the 22.02.86 and was sentenced to 18 years imprisonment by HH Judge Trump. According to probation records the value of the drugs was estimated as being in the region £300, 000; the Judge was recorded as expressing the view that those who import heroin import death and that Mr Aylin was an organiser of the venture. The sentence was nevertheless later reduced to 14 years.

5.2. Mr Aylin maintains he got involved in this offence because he desperately needed money, after experiencing gambling losses. He denies having been the organiser of the importation of the drugs and states he went along with his co-defendant thinking that they were bringing in cannabis to the country.

5.3. On the 28.04.96, Mr Aylin was sentenced to 6 years custody for possession of 120 grams of heroin, with intent to supply. Scales and £1,710 in cash were also found by the police. Whilst Mr Mehmet-Ali accepts that he was found in possession of the heroin, cash and scales, he says, he was asked by a friend to look after these unexpectedly in return for a payment of £1,000. He maintains that he never had any intention of supplying others with the drug and that he had never done so. Judge Finn took the view that Mr Aylin had made money from trafficking in drugs and made a Confiscation Order of £8,500. Of serious concern, is that this offence was committed whilst Mr Aylin had been released from Prison on Parole and this factor should perhaps most certainly, exclude him from being released on Parole on this occasion.

5.4. Mr Aylin now states that he was very foolish to have got involved in both offences. The second offence resulted in him being recalled back to Prison. He tells me that he has never used illegal substances himself. He believes his main motive was to make money, but that this was "fool's gold" which in reality resulted in him being incarcerated for a lengthy period and his family suffering during this time. He conveys that he no longer has a gambling addiction. However, I believe his behaviour would need to me monitored and that any gambling should not be permitted if released on parole as a precaution. It is also apparent that he now deeply regrets his actions. He relates that a number of people in the Turkish community in the North London area have been involved in dealing with heroin. He states that his involvement was peripheral and that he and these other people treated it, as if it were a business, with few concerns about the effects on addicts and society in general. He believes that he was "set up" by his former friend regarding the second offence, as this person was not arrested, even though he believes the Police must have witnessed him pass the package to him. As a result of his experiences, he says he is now extremely mistrustful of those involved in these illegal activities and says he wants nothing to do with such people. He relates that most of them have now been arrested by the police and are currently serving lengthy prison sentences. Since his last sentence, he states that he has had opportunity to consider the impact of drugs on individuals and society. Whilst in prison, he has participated in an offending behaviour group, where he has heard at first hand the experiences of those who have suffered as a result of addictions to drug misuse. He says he now recognises the high level of crime caused by drugs and the damage done to individuals through being addicted.

6 Local community's attitude to offender

6.1. No adverse reaction to his release appears likely. He is not a high- profile offender and has served a lengthy sentence.

7 Whereabouts of any former co-accused or associates

7.1. According to Mr Aylin the majority are all serving prison sentences. Nevertheless, this issue remains a concern to me and particularly what occurred when he was last released on Parole. My advice to him would be, that he should, if possible, consider making a completely fresh start in a different area from where he was previously.

8 Risk to the Public of Reoffending

8.1. It is of concern, that Mr Aylin has two convictions for serious offences, both of which involved a class A drug, heroin. To make matters worse, Mr Aylin committed the last offence whilst he was on parole. From what he tells me, at the time, he was last released on Parole, he considered himself as an outsider of normal society and says he cared little about the consequences to others of heroin misuse. He states that he has now moved on and is motivated towards ensuring that he never reoffends. He says that as a result of the offending behaviour group in custody, and his discussions with probation officers, he is now much more concerned and aware of the terrible impact of drugs on others. However, he acknowledges that he may be considered as unsuitable, on this occasion, due to his previous breach of Parole.

8.2. Mr Aylin appears to have used his time in custody to take steps to improve himself and to address his offending behaviour. He appears motivated to avoid re- offending for the sake of his family. He has served a long sentence and is well aware of the negative impact that this has had upon his family and seems keen to play a positive role as a responsible parent in future.

9 Likely response to Supervision

9.1. His periods of home leave with his family appear to have gone well and he has reported properly as instructed to the Probation Office whilst on leave. My experience of him to date, is that he will make good use of supervision to discuss his past offending behaviour, his concerns surrounding his family and his future plans towards leading a constructive life without crime. My impression is that he would co-operate fully with Probation.

10 Conclusion

10.1. Mr Aylin has been involved in most serious offences. Whilst he recognises that they were very serious offences, it may be that he has attempted to minimise his involvement. This minimisation is of serious concern to me, as it could and perhaps even should prevent his release on Parole in most instances, both on the last occasion he was released on Parole but also this. However, whereas in the past when it seemed he cared little about the impact of drugs on others, it is apparent to me, that he is now well aware of the terrible effects, that he cares about this and expresses appropriate remorse. He is also well aware and ashamed of the way his ex-partner and the children have all suffered as a result of his imprisonment. He appears well motivated towards ensuring that he does not re-offend for the sake of his family and appears keen to forge a positive role for himself with them. He is conscious of the consequences of breaching his licence and seems unlikely to risk another return to custody. He also appears motivated to co-operate fully with Probation, whilst under supervision.

10.2. All things considered; in the unlikely event that the Parole Board decides to excuse his apparent minimisation of his involvement in the original offences and his previous breach of Parole, I would propose that this man should be granted parole. If granted, the aims of supervision would be:

- To monitor his future behaviour and maintain his motivation towards avoiding offending.

- To ban him from engaging all forms of gambling activities and that should he engage in any form of gambling he be recalled back to Prison.

- To ensure he remains fully aware of the consequences of offending on his family.

- To educate him further about the terrible impact of drugs on individuals. With this in mind arrangements would be made for him to meet with a drug counsellor from Turning Point for discussions about the impact of heroin on individuals

- To ensure that he makes a complete fresh start in

the community with absolutely no contact with any of his former criminal associates.

- To assist him re-establish himself into society and to help ensure he returns to legitimate employment as soon as possible

- To supervise him strictly in accordance with National Standards laid down by the Home Office.

10.3. However, it seems possible that he is not granted Parole on this occasion and should this be the case, I would respectfully suggest that he be granted additional Home Leaves to enable him to prepare for his eventual release next year.

John Ebrington
Probation Officer
16.06.98

Section 25

Police Corruption and Crimes Committed by Police Officers
Commentary on Parole Report

Mr Aylin was not granted Parole, but he was granted additional Home Leaves as I had requested. I was not sure whether to believe Mr Aylin about being set up by his friend, when last released on Parole and his account of it seemed a bit strange. I therefore asked him about it, when he next came in on Home Leave from prison.

He explained that not long after his release on Parole, he said his friend contacted him on the telephone and asked him to look after a small quantity of drugs for him, in return for a payment of £1,000.

They arranged to meet at a petrol station, where his friend would hand over the package to him. Once he arrived at the petrol station, within seconds of the package being handed over to him, the police swooped in and arrested him for being in possession of the package. Inside the package, there were more drugs and money than that his friend had told him would be there. Also, there were some scales which had not been previously mentioned by his so called- "friend." This made him suspicious.

He was also suspicious by how quickly the police had swooped in and arrested him. He concluded that it all happened so fast, that the Police must have been watching and seen the package being passed to him by his so called "friend." And yet, his friend had not been arrested. Mr Aylin felt that this indicated that his so called "friend" and the police officer in charge of his arrest, were working together and had both set him up together.

I questioned their possible motives for doing this. Mr Aylin told me, that he had heard, that this particular, police officer, had been working closely with that particular "drug dealing family". Not only was he apparently being paid cash by them, but he was also going around arresting anyone not linked to the family, who attempted to deal drugs within the drug dealing family's territory. He arrested so many, that he appeared to be some sort of supercop.

"But why did they want to set up Mr Aylin?" I questioned. Mr Aylin said he wasn't sure, but he said that he felt that his former friend may have been stopped with the drugs and scales and that the police officer chose to get rid of them, by passing them onto him. Or perhaps, maybe his friend's drug family, saw him as some sort of threat, when he was released on parole.

I just felt that there was more going on than Mr Aylin was letting on. But what was clear about it, was that Mr Aylin was upset about it all and he said he wanted revenge upon the "drug dealing family." He said that he had a lot of information about this family and that he would like to tell the authorities about them.

I made it plain that I felt that Mr Aylin had made a huge mistake in having any-thing to do with that family when he was released upon parole. He should have put the phone down upon them. You need to lead a squeaky-clean life, when released upon parole and have nothing to do with crime.

However, I was sympathetic about his idea about telling the authorities about this drug dealing family. Having seen the awful misery and havoc caused by illegal substances, I felt it would be good to see a major criminal drug group taken out.

I told Mr Aylin that I would like to assist him if I could. I did have contacts within the Police, but that these were at pretty low level. Mr Aylin told me that he felt that would be no good, as there was a police officer involved and he said he felt uncertain how to proceed.

Months passed and when he next came to see me, he was all upbeat and positive.

"I have found a way," he told me, "I have contacted the Customs and Excise and they have taken up the case. They have already moved in on the family who own a travel agency and a garage and have had them both closed down for V A T evasion. The family used to launder all of their proceeds of crime through their travel agency and their garage."

"Oh, that is interesting," I said, "But what about the corrupt Police Officer. What did they say about that?"

"They told me not to worry about it, as they said that they have to deal with situations like that all of the time. They said that the main thing is that they are going to take good care of me. Sooner or later, they are going to move in on that family." said Mr Aylin.

Suddenly, he turned to the map on the wall and said, "One of them lives just here." He pointed to a residential street on the map, "You cover that area, don't you? Wouldn't it be funny if you got him!" he said and laughed.

Following this, Mr Aylin came in for one final appointment with me after he had been released from Prison and come to the end of his sentence. As he had come to the end of his sentence, he no longer needed to be supervised by me. He told me that he was moving away to live somewhere in rural Wales where he was going to run a Chicken Farm. It was somewhere in the country-side, where he said no-one would be able to find him.

It all happened so quickly, that I think he was being relocated with a new identity to a new area by the authorities and I wished him well.

A couple of years later, I was asked to travel up to interview someone in Prison for a Court Report and I had forgotten all about what Mr Aylin had told me. The Court Report was concerning a massive drug bust, conducted by Customs and Excise and the National Police Crime Agency, when 20 kilos of drugs were found in a car in a lock up garage, worth an estimated 2 million pounds and a further 100 kilos of Heroin estimated to be worth 10 million pounds that was found at a residential house nearby. The man I was interviewing, was arrested at the lock up garage and admitted being in possession of the 2 million pounds worth of heroin. He was very glib about the offence, as he conveyed, he had very limited involvement and knew very little about it. He maintained he did not know anyone else involved. When I asked him about his employment history, he told me that he used to work at the family travel agency and garage, until they were closed down by Customs and Excise for VAT evasion.

"Where is it you live?" I asked the offender, who gave me the name of the street that Mr Aylin had pointed to, on the map in my office. It was a good thing that Mr Aylin was now hidden away somewhere in the country-side, where no one could find him.

Some worrying things offenders used to say about the Police.

It was not uncommon for offenders to say that they had been assaulted by the police. One man who had been dealing in drugs, recounted that when his home was raided by the police, about £12,000 in cash was found hidden in the loft. But by the time the matter got to Court the amount found by the police had reduced to £6,000. The offender said that he was not going to advise the Court otherwise. What was concerning was that there were other similar accounts of this sort of thing happening from other offenders, but should they be believed?

The Court Reports I wrote about Police Officers who broke the law.

There were several. One was a man who had got quite burnt out on the job. He had been a murder detective and kept getting flashbacks of some of the dead bodies he had delt with, particularly those earlier in his career. He also developed a drink problem and became addicted to alcohol. He was caught drink driving. He told me that he had been stopped a couple of times previously when the police officers stopping him let him off, on account of him being a police officer.

There was another case, that I delt with, which has been in the media and I shall decline mentioning his name. Over a period of about 15 months, he spent £73,000 on a credit card issued to him to use for expenses, except most of the money was not spent on legitimate expenses, but on buying items for his girlfriend and numerous drinks for his colleagues. This man clearly had problems, which I think his superiors, should have picked up upon. Also, at the time the Met Police's management of expenses appears to have been totally and utterly incompetent. His was not an isolated case and if any- thing, it would appear he was possibly made an example of.

I highly recommend reading investigative reporter Tom Harper's Book, *"Broken Yard. The fall of the Metropolitan Police"*, which details what was happening at that time. It describes the Met Polce auditors expressing alarm about 3500 corporate credit cards being issued to counter -terrorist officers with few checks on the money being spent. To quote directly from the book, one of the auditors said in 2006, "There are 3,500 cards, we've spent £8.5 million and we can only account for £3.5 million".

This means that £5 million of tax payers' money could not be accounted for by the Met Police, which I think was an absolute scandal. That means that £5 million of tax payers' money was not spent appropriately. On closer examination, Tickner the chief auditor said in the book, "One of them had paid off his gambling debts- about eighty grand's worth. Another had been using it to enhance his wife's breasts. £13,500 was spent on the surgery!" Only a handful of the officers were apparently pursued as the numbers were too big to handle according to the book. In my opinion, what an absolute disgrace.

According to Tom Harper's book there were expense abuses going on in other police departments too. In his book Tom Harper quotes Special Branch protection officer's Ron Evans' memoires. *"By the time I joined Special Branch and first went out of town, I witnessed the corruption that went on from all the ranks. Buying alcohol, meals for the wives and girlfriends was the norm. I knew what all of us were doing was wrong and in those early days I knew that this shouldn't be happening and I should do something about it. But it was so endemic and, being a very junior officer, having just joined one of the most specialist departments in any police force, I kept quiet. In my naivety, I thought that because so many other officers were swimming in the same pool as me, all that would happen was that the job would ask me to resign and go quietly."*

In his book, Tom Harper explains that although a significant number of firearms officers were found to be not following correct procedures, with their expenses it was decided to pursue just one single officer and that was Ron Evans, who was furious about it.

Even more concerning, are the police officers who have been found to have been committing serious offences. Met Police officer Wayne Couzens was in 2021 convicted of Murder, kidnapping and rape of a young woman who he had stopped and identified himself as a police officer and had hand cuffed her and placed in his car. A lot of concern has been expressed over the fact that he had committed a number of alleged sexual offences as a serving police officer that the police had clearly failed to deal with.

Following this, Met Police officer David Carrick was arrested in 2021, for having committed numerous serious sexual offences as a serving police officer. In 2022, he was convicted for 44 serious offences of rape and false imprisonment. Again, very serious concerns must be expressed about the recruitment, selection and management of the police.

Your decision:
Should Mr Aylin be granted Parole?

What did Mr Aylin look like?
He was a big thickset man with silvery hair and a moustache. He looked tired and broken and as if he had aged a lot in Prison. Although he seemed pleasant enough there was something a bit menacing about him. You had a gut feeling about him that you would not want to cross him.

What would you think of this Parole report if you were Mr Aylin?

Do you think that Mr Aylin minimised his involvement in his offending and if so how?

How high is the risk of Mr Aylin reoffending?

Very low / low / medium / high / very high?

What risk of harm does Mr Aylin pose the public?

Very low / low / medium / high / very high?

What do you think is the best way of reducing Mr Aylin offending?

Would you grant Mr Aylin Parole?

What events during Mr Aylin's life do you think have contributed to him becoming an Offender and what things could have helped him not offend?

How would you go about helping someone address a gambling addiction?

Gambling addictions are widespread in the UK, how could we as a society go about reducing this in the UK?

What would you do about Mr Aylin's assertion that he had been set up?

How truthful was Mr Aylin being about being set up?

YOU, THE SENTENCER - WHAT WOULD YOU CHOOSE?

Section 26

Route Map for Tackling Offending

Report 12

Brief Outline of case:

Court Report 12. Magistrates Court.
The defendant is Mark Delta and he is aged 29 years. His offences are Driving whilst disqualified and aggravated taking a vehicle without consent.

Mark Delta was a victim of abuse as a child and since childhood had led a very unsettled existence. Mark Delta has a serious addiction to drugs and is asking for help to address it.

Commentary on report 12.
How would you sentence Mark Delta? There appears to be a common thread of disturbed childhoods and being victims of crime as a child, leading on to becoming offenders. Mark Delta slept in cars when he was homeless. Finally, there is some good news about Mark Delta.

Instructions:
Imagine you are about to sentence Mr Delta

Carefully read through the following report. It is based upon a real person and real events that actually happened. All of the names of people and places have been changed as have some of the details of the defendant so as to protect their identity.

As you carefully read through the report, think about the facts of the case and what happened. Think about the actions of the defendant and the potential impact upon victims. Also carefully consider the defendant's behaviour and attitudes and their background.

Once you have read the report proceed onto the Commentary on Report 12 section and answer all of the questions before sentencing Mr Delta.

Please also give consideration as to what steps society could take towards reducing similar offences happening in future.

THE PROBATION SERVICE

This is a pre-sentence report as defined in Section 3(5) of the Criminal Justice Act 1991, it has been prepared in accordance with the National Standard for pre-sentence reports. It is a confidential document prepared specifically for this court hearing.

MAGISTRATES COURT

Date of Hearing: 3.08. 2002

Full name: Mark Delta
Address: 26, Downtown Road   Lower Ruttlesford

Age: 29 years

Offence
Driving whilst disqualified.
Aggravated taking a vehicle without consent.

Petty sessions area: Ruttlesford

Supervising court: Ruttlesford

Completion date: 1.08.2002

Report Produced by: Mr John Ebrington
official title: Probation Officer

Address:
Probation Office, Civic Centre Ruttlesford Home County   RU23 8P

1 Introduction

1.1. To prepare this report I was given Papers from the Crown Prosecution Service, but these did not include witness statements. I was also given the defendant's list of previous convictions; however, these appear to be incorrect as some of his previous convictions that both he and the probation service are aware of do not appear on the list. I held an interview with the defendant at the Probation Office. I have had access to Probation Service records regarding his previous periods of supervision, when he was supervised by the Borough Probation office. I have also had a discussion with his previous supervising officer at Borough, Peter Howard.

2 Offence analysis

2.1. The Court has indicated that it is taking a serious view of these offences and has asked that "All Options" including a custodial sentence be considered. Police attending an alarm call in Barnard Cross saw the defendant driving a car in the vicinity. On seeing the police, he sped off. He went down a cull- de- sac and hit a parked car, causing damage to it. He then decamped from the vehicle and ran off, but was eventually caught by the police. When searched he was found to have a small amount of cannabis in his possession.

2.2. The car had previously been stolen from the station

car park at Hamden Grove. The defendant admits buying this car from a "friend" and that he realised that it may have been stolen because the ignition had been tampered with and the price was cheap.

2.3. Mr Delta told me that he had purchased the car so as to enable him to travel to work. He said that following his last release from custody, he had gone to live with an old school friend and her family. He described how in his view; the family had gone through a difficult period and he had tried to be supportive of them. He said that following the father's death after an illness with cancer, the mother was also diagnosed to be suffering with cancer. He told me that he had overheard her expressing the view that she wished he would get a job. He conveyed that he felt indebted to this family and had to get a job. After finding work, he said that he purchased the car to get him to and from his place of employment.

2.4. The Crown Prosecution papers do not give details of how much damage was done to the parked car and the costs of the repair. From the victim's point of view, it can be extremely annoying to have one's parked car hit by an uninsured vehicle, rendering any claim complex and often the cost of insurance being increased.

2.5. The defendant's actions were clearly premeditated. Mr Delta's lengthy list of previous convictions; the fact that he was apparently knowingly driving a stolen vehicle, the fact that he tried to get away from the police and the damage done to the victim's car are all factors that tend to heighten the seriousness of his offence.

2.6. Mr Delta told me he is aware of the serious view the Courts take of this type of offence and of the risks it poses to the public. He conveyed that he genuinely feels ashamed of his actions and that he has a very low opinion of himself. He explained that he had been offending since he was of a young age, that it had become a way of life for him and one that he would like to break. He said that offending had routinely become a means to an end and that often, he had not cared about what might happen to him. However, he confessed to feeling highly anxious on this occasion and said that he did not understand why this was the case.

3   Offender Assessment

3.1. Mr Delta has a long list of previous convictions since 1989. These have been dealt with by means of conditional discharges, fines, probation, community service and imprisonment. The persistent nature of his offending has resulted in him being sentenced to terms of imprisonment on some 15 occasions and no noticeable reduction in his offending behaviour. In particular, Mr Delta has some 13 previous convictions for Driving whilst Disqualified.

Alongside these are two convictions for Dangerous Driving and one for Aggravated Vehicle Taking. The last occasion he was before the courts was in November last year, when he was sentenced to a custodial sentence for an offence of Driving whilst Disqualified.

3.2. The defendant is an only child and I understand that his father died before he was born. He recounts that he had a close relationship with his mother and a reasonably happy childhood up until the age of 14. At this age, his mother formed a relationship with a man who later became his stepfather. Mr Delta did not get on with his stepfather and states that he was subjected to severe physical abuse. As a result, Mr Delta began to spend more time away from home, truanted from school and became involved with petty theft and drug use. He said he hung around in parks and went to stay with different people. He confided, that men, sexually abused him on three separate occasions during this period. He said that he had never told any-one about this before. Based on the information he gave me, I have no reason to doubt his account, which corresponds with the Probation Service's knowledge about the victims' perspective of such offending. He recalls eventually leaving home, when he was 15 years old, and began to live with an aunt, for a short time, but subsequently had no stable address.

3.3. Mr Delta failed to complete his GCSE examinations,

though he recalls that he had performed well in his mock examinations. He tells me that he did not approach Social Services when he left home, because he did not want to hurt his mother. He conveys that he feels he has achieved very little since first leaving home. He no longer has any contact with his mother.

3.4. Despite the persistent nature of his offending, there appears to be a gap between 1993 and 1995 when he was not offending. At the time, he was subject to a Probation Order and appeared to be making progress. He was in a settled relationship, had obtained regular employment and was living in rented accommodation. This settled period came to an end following the loss of his job, a separation with his girlfriend and the loss of his accommodation. Following this, his drug use appears to have increased partly as a means of coping with his depression.

3.5. Mr Delta tells me that, from a young age, he has regularly used amphetamines and cannabis. Although he has experimented with other drugs, he says that he does not use heroin or cocaine. Mr Delta tells me that he continues to use amphetamines, as a prop to help him overcome feelings of inferiority and lack of self-confidence, when dealing with others. He states his addiction is such that he cannot function normally without the drug. He also believes that the abuse he suffered as a child may be a contributory factor in the difficulties he has since experienced in maintaining a law-abiding life-style.

3.6. Mr Delta states that he has largely spent unproductive periods in custody. Nevertheless, I am advised that he completed examinations in English, Maths and Pottery, and an NVQ qualification in Information Technology. He has also attended a drug rehabilitation course whilst in custody, I understand he underwent a psychiatric assessment during a recent term of imprisonment and was diagnosed as being clinically depressed.

3.7. From his account, Mr Delta has experienced an unsettled existence following his releases from imprisonment. He states that the custodial sentences often resulted in him losing his accommodation and employment. He tells me that he was often released homeless. He maintains that he used to purchase cars on occasion to live in and that this then resulted in a number of Drive whilst Disqualified convictions. Records confirm that he has in the past worked as a roofer and in other casual employment. For a period, he worked as a fireplace fitter on a casual basis. Currently, he works as a labourer for a landscape gardener. However, he says that he has no job security, as it is only temporary. As previously stated, he currently lives with his friend's mother. He contributes towards the housekeeping and seems to appreciate being in a family environment.

3.8. Mr Delta was subject to a Community Rehabilitation Order for a short period in 2001. However, the order was revoked when he re-offended only three months after the imposition of the Order. Records indicate that he reported satisfactorily during the period. As part of the Order, he was due to attend a Drive whilst Disqualified programme, but was unable to complete this, due to his custodial sentence. He says he appreciated the drug counselling that he received, but found that its availability was limited, as the counsellor had many other people to see. He recalls a positive experience of being on a Community Rehabilitation Order and that he responded to the disciplined approach adopted by his officer. However, quite unprompted, he says in his own words, that he felt "Probation supervision" was too limited and that he could benefit from a more structured and intensive regime.

3.9. A screening for literacy and numeracy suggests that Mr Delta has no problems with these.

4 Assessment of the Risk of Harm to the Public and Likelihood of Reoffending

4.1. Mr Delta has a lengthy and appalling record of previous convictions. They tend to fall into two categories; crimes of dishonesty, committed to fund his substance misuse, and motoring offences such as Driving whilst Disqualified. It should be noted however, that despite his dreadful record of previous convictions, he has never been convicted for offences of violence against the person, domestic burglary or offences such as robbery. Nevertheless, Mr Delta's record of persistent offending suggests that he is at high risk of reoffending and in my opinion, he poses a potential risk to the public on the roads, through committing further driving offences.

4.2. Mr Delta has a long history of serious amphetamine misuse. He appears to have a chronic addiction to the drug and seems unable to function without it. He seems to use the drug to mask his feelings of depression, insecurity and debilitating low self-esteem. In my view, much of his offending is linked to his substance-misuse and his exceptionally negative outlook on life. His behaviour seems almost self-destructive at times. In the past, he has not cared about what sentence the Court has meted out and repetitive Custodial sentences have not deterred him from reoffending. In my opinion, the key issue in trying to tackle this man's offending behaviour would be to address both his substance-misuse and his depression. This seems unlikely to be achieved in my opinion on a normal Community Rehabilitation Order and I think that Mr Delta is quite right in expressing the view that he needs something more structured and intensive.

In my opinion, a Drug Treatment and Testing Order would provide the Courts with the best option of reducing this man's offending behaviour. The treatment providers, Dole House, whilst addressing his substance-misuse problem have access to the services of a psychiatrist, as required, and I feel that this would be particularly helpful in this case.

5 Conclusion

5.1. This offence is 'so serious,' that it seems fairly inevitable that the Court will be considering a custodial sentence today. However, such a measure has not deterred Mr Delta from offending in the past and imprisonment has often had a negative impact upon him by rendering him homeless.

5.2. The Court does have the option of imposing a Curfew Order in this case. Mr Delta advises me that there would be no problem in the monitoring equipment being installed at the address where he is residing.

5.3. Whilst Mr Delta is assessed as suitable for a Community Punishment Order, I feel that I must express grave concerns about his substance-misuse and the possibility of him re offending during the currency of the Order.

5.4. Whilst, Mr Delta would be suitable for the imposition of a Community Rehabilitation Order, I believe that the intensive and structured approach of the Drug Treatment and Testing Order is much more likely to have a longer lasting impact upon the defendant's offending behaviour.

5.5. If the Court is able to consider an alternative to custody, I would suggest that this case be adjourned for a two- week period to enable Mr Delta to be fully assessed. During the two weeks he would be expected to attend a series of interviews which would test out his motivation and commitment to the programme.

John Ebrington
Probation Officer

Section 27

A Problematic Childhood Can Lead to Becoming an Offender

Commentary Court Report 12

Outcome of Case

Mark Delta's case was adjourned for a (DTTO) Drug Treatment and Testing Order assessment which he successfully completed. He was eventually sentenced to a two- year DTTO which went really well indeed.

A year or so later his Probation Officer Sarah Whitehaven told me how well he had been doing on his DTTO. She said that I had written an excellent report and that it had acted as a spring-board for him to do well on the Order, which was very kind of her. However, report I think was more down to him as it was just a reflection of his readiness for positive change at the time. He also had a stable home life which I think was very helpful to him.

The DTTO was a new scheme which had been introduced at around that time that was significantly better than was available a few years previously. You will see in the next report what went on before and that it was fairly hopeless.

I really liked the DTTO. The first thing to note about it, was that the DTTO was held by the court that imposed it and the defendant used to have to return to Court for regular reviews of the offender's progress on the order. A short review report would be prepared by the Probation Officer detailing all of the drug test results and the defendant's progress on the various elements of the programme. The Magistrates or the Judge would ask questions, make comment and often would motivate the offender. My impression was that the sentencers seemed to enjoy taking part in the process.

The whole review process used to make the offenders and me very motivated. I recall on the occasions I attended I had to be ready to field any questions from the sentencers which was challenging. The sentencers seemed to enjoy the process. I recall that the Judges used to make a point of removing their wigs for these reviews because it wasn't a formal hearing.

Drug Testing Regime
The whole object of the Order was to gradually wean people off drugs, reduce reoffending and it has proven quite successful regards this. Some magistrates expected people to test negative immediately over- night, but of course it takes time to come off drug addictions and it is much better that people test honestly.

The drug tests were done twice per week for the first 13 weeks. Normally these would be urine tests or occasionally saliva tests. They have also been developing a bracelet that is worn and that can detect alcohol and drug use.

I remember people drinking lots of water before doing their urine tests. I think they were trying to water down their drug levels. One guy spent ages standing in front of the urinal stating he couldn't pee. His test came back that it could not have been produced by a human being, as contained 100% water. It seems he was standing there for ages waiting for the urinal to flush. I half expected for him to have a small running bottle of his girlfriend's pee stuffed down his trousers next time and for the test to come back that he was pregnant.

I think that people trying to cheat the tests was exceptionally rare. There was no point trying to do it and the saliva tests were much easier to administer if required to do so.

Mark Delta eventually came off drugs and stopped offending altogether upon successfully completing his Drug Treatment and Testing Order.

Sentencing Mark Delta

What did Mark Delta look like?
Mark Delta looked like a man ready to go and work outside and do landscape gardening. He had check lumberyard type jacket and big boots. He lowered his eyes at times in conversation and presented as being of low self-esteem. He was fairly quiet and unassuming and seemed sincere when he spoke.

> What would you think of this Court report if you were Mr Delta?
>
> What significant events happened to Mark Delta when he was a teenager?
>
> How many times has Mark Delta been sentenced to terms of imprisonment?
>
> He was often homeless following his release from Prison. What did he sometimes sleep in when he was homeless?
>
> What did Mark Delta say he felt was lacking about Probation?
>
> How high is the risk of Mr Delta reoffending?
>
> Very low / low / medium / high / very high?

What risk of harm does Mr Delta pose the public?

Very low / low / medium / high / very high?

What do you think is the best way of reducing Mr Delta offending?

How would you sentence Mr Delta?

What events during Mr Delta's life do you think have contributed to him becoming an Offender and what things could have helped him not offend?

Many offenders appear to have experienced problematic childhoods. How can we as a society try to reduce the numbers of problematic childhoods occurring in the UK?

What steps could society take to reduce Driving Whilst Disqualified offences?

How can the UK reduce illegal drug taking in the UK?

YOU, THE SENTENCER - WHAT WOULD YOU CHOOSE?

Section 28

Low Depths of Drug Addictions
Report 13

Brief Outline of case:

Court Report 13. Magistrates Court.
The defendant is David Howe who is aged 25 years. His offences are theft of jewellery and watches and obtaining £50 and £40 by deception.

David Howe stole from his own family in order to feed his drug habit. He obtained money from his father's account by forging his father's signature. He was asked to leave home after this.

Commentary on report 13.
How would you sentence David Howe? Prior to the introduction of Drug Treatment and Testing Orders, trying to help offenders address their drug addictions in the 1990's was extremely difficult. Prison sentences were not always helpful. David Howe was introduced to Heroin and became addicted to it whilst in Prison. David Howe asked for help from his own GP who turned

him away. He nevertheless found support from another GP. Community resources to address addictions were extremely limited during the 1990's.

Instructions:
Imagine you are about to sentence Mr Howe.

Carefully read through the following report. It is based upon a real person and real events that actually happened. All of the names of people and places have been changed as have some of the details of the defendant so as to protect their identity.

As you carefully read through the report, think about the facts of the case and what happened. Think about the actions of the defendant and the potential impact upon victims. Also carefully consider the defendant's behaviour and attitudes and their background.

Once you have read the report, proceed onto the Commentary on Report 13 section and answer all of the questions before sentencing Mr Howe.

Please also give consideration as to what steps society could take towards reducing similar offences happening in future.

THE PROBATION SERVICE

This is a pre-sentence report as defined in Section 3(5) of the Criminal Justice Act 1991, it has been prepared in accordance with the National Standard for pre-sentence reports. It is a confidential document prepared specifically for this court hearing.

MAGISTRATES COURT

Date of Hearing: 3.01. 1999

Full name: David Howe
Address: 28, Downtrodden Road   Middle Ruttlesford

age: 25 years

Offence
Theft of jewellery and watches and
obtaining £50 and £40 by deception.

petty sessions area: Ruttlesford

supervising court: Ruttlesford

Completion date: 02.01.1999

Report Produced by: Mr John Ebrington
official title: Probation Officer

Address: Probation Office, Civic Centre Ruttlesford   RU23 8P

1   **Introduction**

1.1. This report is based on my knowledge of Mr Howe as his supervising Probation Officer. He was made subject to a Probation Order in June 1998. I have held an interview in addition to normal supervision in order to specifically address these offences and Mr Howe's Probation Records which include his record of previous convictions. I have liaised with Mr Rupert White, substance misuse counsellor of Turning Point and with Mr Howe's GP who has written a letter to the Court about Mr Howe, but I have not seen yet.

2   **Offence Analysis**

2.1. Mr Howe was at the time of these offences living with his father. He stole items of jewellery, worth £1,200, which had previously belonged to his deceased mother. These were taken to Cash Converters where Mr Howe received £150 for the items with an option to buy them back within 28 days for £190. About a week later, Mr Howe withdrew funds from his father's building society account; £40 on one day and then £50 the following day, by forging his father's signature. The building society confiscated the book when Mr Howe made a third attempt to dishonestly withdraw money from his father's account. Following this, he wrote a letter to his father outlining his offences and apologising for his actions. It is apparent from the witness statements, that Mr Howe made full admissions to the police when he was interviewed by them. However, he informed the police that he had paid back £90 to his father from his giro, but his father disputes this.

2.2. These offences are most serious. Mr Howe breached his father's trust and irrespective of the financial value, the jewellery must have been of great sentimental value to Mr Howe senior. Furthermore, these offences were premeditated and involved a degree of sophistication, in the way that Mr Howe forged his father's signature to dishonestly obtain the money from the account. This said, Mr Howe promptly admitted the offences and apologised to his father. He also co-operated fully with the police. I understand that the items of jewellery have now been recovered.

2.3. It is relevant to point out at this stage, that Mr Howe is a man who has been trying to address his addiction to heroin mis-use over the past few years. He tells me that his father used to try to assist him to overcome his addiction. Mr Howe explains that at the time of this offence, he had relapsed into heroin mis-use and his motivation for committing the offences was to clear his drug debt. He says that he feels disgusted with himself for having committed these offences. He explains that his intention in stealing funds from his father's account was to try to recover the jewellery from the shop. Mr Howe expresses deep regret that his relationship with his father is now over and states that he now feels that he will now have to mature and quickly learn to stand on his own two feet, without his father's support. His father has found a new partner and Mr Howe feels that this has been a factor in the relationship ending. He adds that he feels his father has been untruthful to the police and exaggerated the value of the jewellery taken as a way of ending their relationship for good. However, he states that he ultimately blames himself for the break-up of his relationship with his father and describes feeling that he is going some kind of grieving process over it.

3   Relevant information about the offender

3.1. Mr Howe first experimented with drugs and alcohol when he was about 11 years old. Although he tried most drugs as a teenager, he says he did not like the majority of them and tended to abuse alcohol, from time to time and smoke cannabis. It was not until 1994 that he was first introduced to heroin, when he was remanded in prison for an assault offence. Upon learning that his mother was terminally ill with cancer, he had gone out, got drunk and then assaulted someone. He was sentenced to two-years, Probation with a condition that he attend the anger management group.

3.2. Mr Howe responded well to Probation. He reported as instructed and made good use of supervision, when he was given assistance to try to come to terms with his mother's terminal illness and her eventual death. At the time, his Probation Officer expressed the view that Mr Howe had difficulties in discussing his feelings and that this had sometimes led to frustration and aggressive ways. He attended the anger management group and is said to have participated well. By the end of the programme, he was assessed as being more able to recognise what made him angry and to consider his actions before losing his temper.

3.3. Shortly after his release from custody, Mr Howe stopped using heroin by his own efforts. Although he had been an illegal driver in the past, he took and passed his driving test during this period. He gained employment with a demolition firm and trained and qualified in driving the variety of specialist vehicle's that they use.

3.4. However, early in 1997 he started to use heroin again. He says that the drug was very accessible and became tempted to use it, when he saw his friends with it. Although he had used in different ways in the past, on this occasion, he began injecting himself. Not before long, he became addicted and lost his job because of his drug mis-use. Whereas he had found it relatively easy to stop taking the drug in the past, on this occasion, he has found it very difficult. He recalls going to see his GP, but says he seemed unhelpful about his problem. Then in May

1997, he contacted the Ruttlesford Community Drug Team and was advised that there was a ten to twelve month waiting list for the methadone reduction programme. He recalls becoming despondent and his addiction worsening. By the middle of 1997, he estimates he was using half a gramme of heroin each day and spending approximately £300 to £400 per week.

3.5. Mr Howe was convicted of two offences of theft from shops and in June 1998, he was made subject to a Probation Order with a condition that he participate in a programme designed to reduce his dependency on drugs in conjunction with Turning point. Prior to the imposition of the Order Mr Howe had taken steps to begin addressing his drug problem by registering with another GP, Dr Can, in Broadway, who was prepared to put him on a programme of treatment for heroin abuse. The role of the Probation Service has been to encourage Mr Howe to stick to the programme and he has been given specialist counselling from Mr Rupert White of Turning Point.

3.6. Mr Howe has been prescribed methadone, anti-depressants and sleeping pills. At the outset of treatment, he was prescribed 50 ml of methadone per day and this was reduced to 15ml and then 5 ml per day last October. Mr Howe has regularly attended his probation appointments as instructed, and has made good use of supervision to discuss his problems openly. He has found it tremendously hard to address his addiction and has experienced several relapses which left him feeling deeply ashamed, and disgusted with himself. At about that time he learnt that his girlfriend was pregnant and he says he persuaded her to have an abortion, because he did not want a child who would have a father who was a drug addict. Mr Howe has remained medically unfit to work, throughout the period and this has left him feeling frustrated, as he used to enjoy his job. However, Mr Howe currently seems much more positive and focussed in his ability to address his addiction. He tells me that since his remand in HMP Hardcastle in November 1998 for offences of offensive weapon, he has come off drugs altogether and is now no longer taking methadone. Mr Howe is currently living at a friend's house, after being asked to leave his father's home. He says his friend, is an ex-addict who is giving him encouragement. However, how long Mr Howlett can continue staying with his friend, is uncertain and Mr Howe's relationship with his girlfriend has now ended. Mr Howe says he is finding it difficult to cope on his own.

4 Risk to the public of reoffending

4.1 Mr Howe does have a record of having committed serious and violent offences over the years. Nevertheless, the frequency of his offending and the seriousness of his offences does appear to be reducing. The risk of him committing a violent offence appears to have reduced significantly, but nevertheless remains. Mr Howe sometimes presents as being a tough individual and the scar on his face tends to accentuate this image of himself. However, he gained the scar in an accident and during supervisory sessions I have witnessed the emotional and sensitive side of Mr Howe, which he does not normally portray in public. In my opinion, he still does not appear to have got over the death of his mother. He also seems to be a man of low self-esteem, who feels frustrated with himself for being unable to work and who is disgusted with himself for the way his drug addiction has led to his bad behaviour and deceitful manner towards his father and his girlfriend. During supervision, I have been impressed by Mr Howe's determination in trying to overcome his addiction and believe that Probation in partnership with Turning Point has assisted him in maintaining his motivation to try to stop using drugs. I fear he is at risk of relapse and therefore believe that a period in a drug rehabilitation centre, would assist him to learn new ways of coping without drugs. I think that a period in such a centre would assist him to come to terms with his mother's death and to learn to be less dependent on his father and girlfriend. Mr Howe agrees with me and appears motivated to co-operate.

5   Conclusion

5.1. Mr Howe acknowledges the seriousness of his offences and that he is at risk of receiving a custodial sentence. Whilst he conveys that he would not like to be incarcerated he says that he does not fear going to prison and that he would cope with a sentence without too much difficulty. In some ways, Mr Howe says he would welcome a custodial sentence as a way from getting away from some of the pressures he is currently facing. I am nevertheless concerned that such a measure could disrupt the progress he has already made. Should the Court decide to impose such a sentence, both Mr Howe and myself would ask that his Probation Order not be revoked.

5.2. In considering the community- based disposals there appears to be few options open to the Court. Unfortunately, as Mr Howe is currently on sickness benefit and medically unfit to work, he is assessed as unsuitable for Community Service. In this case, I propose that the Court defers sentence for a three- month period to enable the Community Drug team to make a full assessment of Mr Howe's suitability for a rehabilitation centre and to make an application for funding for this from the relevant authorities. In three months- time it will be the new financial year which may assist the application.

5.3. I therefore propose that Mr Howe's sentence be deferred for a three- month period to enable the possibility of Mr Howe going to a drug rehabilitation centre to be fully explored. During the period of deferment Mr Howe will be required to:

- Not commit any offences.

- Attend all appointments with the Community Drug Team.

- Cooperate fully with the Probation Service.

John Ebrington
Probation Officer

Section 29

Lack of Resources to Help People With Addictions in the 1990's
Commentary Court Report 13

Outcome of Case

This case was adjourned for a residential Drug Rehabilitation Treatment assessment which he successfully undertook. However, I recall he was not granted funding to go to a residential rehab. Although he was very motivated to go and a rehab offered him very best chances of overcoming his addiction, he didn't get to go. The reason for this was that the funds were very limited and prioritised for the most needy, vulnerable and ill on drugs. I guess he was assessed as being half way there to overcoming his addiction by his own efforts.

It was exceptionally rare for any-one to get funding to go to a residential rehab. It was a shame as the outcomes were often successful and were certainly more successful than people coming off drugs by their own efforts in the community.

When he went back to Court he was sentenced to more Probation and Community Service.

Back in the 1980's
When I joined the Probation Service in the 1980's there was little provision for Drug Treatment and it remained the same for much of the 1990's. At the time that this report was written, towards the end of the 1990's, we had a new facility which was that a Drug Counsellor from Turning Point had been assigned to our office. He was a welcome and much needed addition. The Drug Treatment and Testing Orders were introduced in October 2000 and were a radical improvement on what went on before. In my experience the situation was absolutely dire where I was working in the mid 1990's.

Building Houses out of a Deck of Cards that kept falling down
I recall there were a lot of people with drug issues coming into the Probation Office where I worked in London. It was sad, as there was little support or treatment available to them. The drug counsellor was belatedly appointed towards the end of the 1990's but before that we were left to our own devices.

For those addicted to heroin needing to go on a methadone reduction programme there was an 8-12 month waiting list at the local Community Drugs Team. We would arrange appointments for our offenders to access this treatment, but if they failed to keep any of their appointments they would slip down to the bottom of the waiting-list. It was just like trying to build a house out of a deck of cards that kept falling down. It was very frustrating.

Some people in the Probation Office waiting room were very ill and appeared to be seemingly slowly dying. I recall one man looked 20-30 years older, than his real age. He used to appear to stagger around and conk out of consciousness every now and again. There was little we could do to help these people.

Addictions were really strong and some offended against their own families in order to feed their addictions. I recall one man stole the family TV and then sold it in order to buy drugs. Families ended up having to issue final warnings and then ask their drug addict family member to leave home.

Now faced with homelessness, sadly all too often, the only people that would let them stay at their homes, were normally fellow addicts. Living together seemed to egg each other on with their addictions and to commit even more crimes in order to fund their habits.

Sometimes they would even offend against each other. One man said he was mugged and his drugs stolen from him several times on his way back from buying them. He said this prompted him to always take a knife with him when he bought his drugs. Another time, he said he was sharing a flat with a friend and had a life-threatening drug overdose. He told me that whilst he was unconscious, his friend stole his benefits and then placed him in the block of flats lift, so that someone else would find him and call an ambulance.

However, not all substance misuser addicts scraped around at the bottom of society like an under-class of its own, continually committing theft type crimes in order to fund their habits. There were also some respectable addicts who were sufficiently financially well off enough to buy illegal drugs without committing crimes. Substance misuse in the UK is massive and urgently needs addressing.

The illegal drug world is nevertheless at times a very nasty world indeed. Not far from where I live there have been several drug gang type murder executions. One of the young men I was supervising hobbled in to see me on crutches having managed to fracture both of his ankles. He initially told me that he had accidentally fallen off his 12th floor balcony, but later admitted it wasn't due to an accident. He later explained that some local criminal drug dealers hadn't taken kindly to him selling cannabis to the local college students as it encroached upon their territory. He said they came round to pay him a visit, proceeded to dangle him over the balcony and let go.

SECTION 29

Sentencing Mr Howe

What did David Howe look like?

David Howe was a tall brown- haired man with a scar on his face. He presented as being tired. He was quiet and seemed sincere when he spoke.

What would you think of this Court report if you were Mr Howe?

What significant events happened to Mr Howe in recent years?

Where did Mr Howe first use Heroin?

What happened when Mr Howe asked his original GP for help in dealing with his Heroin addiction?

How long was the waiting list to get on the methadone reduction programme with the Community Drug Team?

How high is the risk of Mr Howe reoffending?

Very low/ low/ medium/ high / very high?

What risk of harm does Mr Howe pose the public?

Very low/ low/ medium/ high / very high?

How would you sentence Mr Howe?

What events during Mr Howe's life do you think have contributed to him becoming an Offender and what things could have helped him not offend?

Up to 50 per cent of all acquisitive crime is committed by those with a heroin or crack cocaine problem. The proportion increases to 70 per cent for shop theft.

What steps could society take to reduce Drug related offending in the UK?

Section 30

A Professional Criminal Has Enough of Committing Crimes and Cooperates with the Police

Report 14

Brief Outline of case:

Court Report 14. Crown Court. Defendant Nigel Summers. Burglary x 2

Nigel Summers considers himself to be a professional criminal who feels he should stop offending. When stolen jewellery was found in a jacket pocket, he admitted that it was him who had committed the burglary of a jewellery shop. He also took the police to where the jewellery was hidden and admitted to other offences he had committed.

Commentary on report 14.

A new intensive supervision scheme that is run in partnership by Probation Service and the Police is discussed. My experience of working in close proximity of the Police is discussed too.

Instructions:

Imagine you are about to sentence Mr Summers.

Carefully read through the following report. It is based upon a real person and real events that actually happened. All of the names of people and places have been changed as have some of the details of the defendant so as to protect their identity.

As you carefully read through the report, think about the facts of the case and what happened. Think about the actions of the defendant and the potential impact upon victims. Also carefully consider the defendant's behaviour and attitudes and their background.

Once you have read the report proceed onto the Commentary on Report 14 section and answer all of the questions before sentencing Mr Summers.

Please also give consideration as to what steps society could take towards reducing similar offences happening in future.

THE PROBATION SERVICE

This is a pre-sentence report as defined in Section 3(5) of the Criminal Justice Act 1991, it has been prepared in accordance with the National Standard for pre-sentence reports. It is a confidential document prepared specifically for this court hearing.

CROWN COURT

Date of Hearing: 3.01. 2003

Full name: Nigel Starmer Summers
Address: 58, Downtrodden Road   Middle Ruttlesford

age: 36 years

Offence: Burglary x2

petty sessions area: Ruttlesford

supervising court: Ruttlesford

Completion date: 02.01.2003

Report Produced by: Mr John Ebrington
official title: Probation Officer

Address: Probation Office, Civic Centre Ruttlesford RU23 8P

1 Introduction

1.1. To prepare this report papers from the Crown Prosecution Service and a list of previous convictions were obtained. One interview with the defendant was held at HMP Snowhill. Probation Service records were looked at concerning previous periods of supervision and discussions were held with his supervising officers. A standard screening for basic literacy and numeracy skills was undertaken.

2 Offence analysis

2.1. The defendant is before the Court for a burglary of a public house and a burglary of a jewellery shop. In addition to this, he has asked for 8 other offences to be taken into consideration. I understand that there is to be a Newton Hearing on two issues; whether or not he entered the dwelling part of the public house, and the value of the jewellery he stole from the shop. Irrespective of the outcome of the Newton Hearing, these would appear to be most serious offences and particularly, in the light of the defendant's record of previous convictions, a custodial sentence would appear inevitable today. Mr Summers was realistic about the prospect when I discussed it with him.

2.2. The landlord of the public house who lived above the premises came downstairs one morning to find that the premises had been broken into via a side window. A forced entry had been made into the fruit machine cash box. The keys to the safe were found and the safe was emptied of cash. The victim also said that he had a set of golf clubs that were stolen. I have not received a list of what was stolen from the public house, or a valuation of how much cash and property was stolen. However, the defendant, in his interview with the police, said that he took approximately £200 from the fruit machine and £1,750 from the safe. In addition to this, he said that he had stolen a number of bottles of spirits. In discussing the victim's perspective of his offence, Mr Summers remained adamant that he did not enter the dwelling part of the public house. He asserted that although he had numerous previous convictions for burglaries, he had never had a conviction for a dwelling and would never do such a thing.

2.3. The burglary of the jewellery shop took place about two weeks later. During the middle of the night, a jewellery shop in Richmond was broken into. The defendant gained access by bashing a hole through a wall on the side of the building. A camera recording revealed an offender moving around the shop apparently avoiding the infrared detectors. A large quantity of Jewellery was stolen. The victim estimates the value to be in the region £222,500. However, the defendant disputed this, stating the value was between £150,000 and £160,000. A search was conducted of the defendant's home about a week later, where upon, the police found a small quantity of the stolen jewellery in his girlfriend's jacket pocket. When questioned by the police, the defendant initially declined to make any comment to them. However, he subsequently admitted the offence and of his own volition showed the police where the remainder of the jewellery was hidden. He advised me that a substantial amount of the items was recovered.

2.4. The 8 offences taken into consideration involve a number of crimes. During April and June 2002, he burgled a local furniture shop, on several occasions and stole a number of items of furniture. In July, he made an attempted burglary of another jewellery shop in Richmond, but apparently gave up trying to gain access, when he had difficulties getting in. However, he also that month broke into a newsagent's shop in Richmond and stole cigarettes and phone cards to the value of £19,150.

2.5. The defendant conveyed that he felt he was in his words, "a career criminal" who had made a determined attempt to stop offending following his last release from prison in 1999. He said that on the strength of this, he was placed on Community Rehabilitation Orders, when he appeared before the Courts in 2001. However, he said that he found himself in tremendous debt in 2002, following an acrimonious divorce and additionally gave up work to look after his son in January this year. He said that he was without furnishings for his flat and stole items so he could furnish it for his son. He said that he started to offend again when his debts got out of control. Whilst expressing regret and remorse for his offences, he seemed to express little empathy for the victims.

3   Offender Assessment

3.1. The defendant is a prolific offender, whose criminal career began at a young age. He experienced considerable violence from his father during his formative years. He dealt with this by running away from home and being taken regularly into the care of Social Services. It was during these adolescent years that he became embroiled in serious crime. He later seemed able to pull away from these negative influences and concentrate on making some success of his own family life. Back in 1988, he began a period in his life when he ceased offending. This was because he had found employment for Bush, in which he progressed to supervising a department. He was proud of his achievement as he was trusted at work, and hoped he could break with offending permanently. However, in 1993 the firm relocated and laid him off and he returned to burglary bitterly insisting he had no other choices. At that time, he felt his poor literacy skills would count against him. However, he improved his reading and writing during his last sentence and now tests as being able.

3.2. Mr Summers met his ex-wife in his late teens and

they were married for some seventeen years; their daughter is aged 18 and their son is 12. Apart from a brief separation during the early 1990s, resulting from his cocaine habit then, their marriage was steady, until his release from custody in August 1999. At this time, he noticed a distinct change in his wife's attitude towards him and they eventually separated permanently in 2001.

3.3. Mr Summers began going to Marlow College in 2000, where he took courses in computer skills. He said that he felt it important that he needed to gain qualifications in order to gain employment and so avoid reoffending. Furthermore, he explained that he had seriously injured himself during a burglary 7 or 8 years ago and had since been unable to undertake hard physical work such as labouring. Whilst at Marlow college, he said that arrangements were made for him to undergo a work experience placement at a residential home for people with dementia. He got on particularly well and was offered a full-time post as a care assistant in 2001. He conveyed that he was grateful to be given the opportunity, as his employers were fully aware of his record of previous convictions. He said that he found the work emotionally challenging and stressful, but also immensely rewarding.

3.4. Mr Summers used to work shifts and said he found it difficult to organise his time to meet his commitment to attend the Think First programme which was a condition of his Community Rehabilitation Orders. He said he found it frustrating having to attend, as he felt it impeded his work and his responsibilities towards his children. Furthermore, he said that he found the content of the programme pathetic, in his view more suited to adolescent offenders, as opposed "career criminals" such as himself. His antipathy was evident during each session of the group. He was apparently dismissive to the point of rudeness and it was felt that his presence was both disruptive and intimidating for the other group members and the leaders. He was returned to Court for breach of the Order, even though he had not accrued any unacceptable absences. He was fined £80 and the condition was removed. Mr Summers expressed his disgust at being breached when I interviewed him at HMP Snowhill and said he felt, he had been treated unfairly and that in his opinion the Probation Service had done little or nothing to help him.

3.5. Both his children opted to live with him, although they both spent considerable periods with their grandmother. He told me that he experienced problems from his ex-partner and that he had to change the locks on the property after he experienced an attack during the night. According to Mr Summers, another problem was that his ex-wife's name remained on the tenancy. He said that she had a number of bad debts and continued to use the address to take out loans, which she subsequently reneged on, resulting in bailiffs coming round. He asked the Probation Service to help him get his tenancy agreement changed and whilst a colleague tried to intervene on his behalf, he became frustrated and angry that the issue was not speedily resolved. When I saw him, he expressed the view that Probation had done nothing to help him about the issue.

3.6. Mr Summers experienced difficulties getting his son into a local school. His Probation Officer attended the appeal panel with him and his appeal was successful. His son came back to live with him, on a permanent basis in December 2001 and he said that as a result he was eventually forced to give up work in order to look after him. Several months later, he began reoffending which led to his current offences.

3.7. Mr Summers has been remanded in custody since August. He was in a relationship with his girlfriend, who lived with him at his flat at the time of the offence. She has since moved out and Mr Summers has lost the tenancy of the property. His son has returned to live with his ex-partner and his daughter is living with her grandmother.

4 Assessment of the Risk of Harm to the Public and Likelihood of Reoffending

4.1. The defendant has an unenviable record of previous convictions that suggest that he is at high risk of offending. He has targeted commercial premises such as jewellery shops in the past and seems at high risk of committing similar offences in future. Although he has gained some five previous convictions for possession of offensive weapons, he has no previous convictions for violent assaults. Nevertheless, his use of weapons is of concern in considering the potential risk to the public, that said, his last such offence was in 1998. He has gained a number of previous convictions for drug related offending. Records reveal that Mr Summers has tended to use drugs during stressful periods in his life, mostly in relation to marital difficulties. However, in the intervening years, Mr Summers managed to remain in control of his drug use and does not feel it was a significant factor in his recent offending. Alcohol is not an issue for him as he states he does not drink.

4.2. Mr Summers' rate of offending seemed to be slowing down in recent years. He also appears to have made a genuine attempt to avoid reoffending following his last release from custody. He took up appropriate steps, such as going to college and finding employment and it is disappointing that he began reoffending this year. He seems to partly blame the Probation Service for this and I fear that this could impact negatively upon his relationship with the Service upon his eventual release.

5   Conclusion

5.1. These offences are so serious that only a custodial sentence would appear appropriate today. Mr Summers informed the police where he had hidden the remainder of the jewellery he had stolen and I would ask that he be given credit for this in determining the length of his sentence. I would also ask that his two existing Community Rehabilitation Orders be revoked in the interests of expediency.

John Ebrington
Probation Officer.

Section 31

A New Scheme Designed to Tackle Persistent Offenders
Commentary Report 14

What was it like to go and interview an offender in Prison?
It was a bit intimidating at first. There were quite a lot of security checks both on the way in to the prison and on the way out. You had to place all of your personal belongings into a locker and you were only allowed to take in a pen, note pad and papers relating to the case. A photo and a finger print were taken of you. Later you were required to put your finger on a machine which flashed up your photo on the guards' TV monitors confirming it was you. There were a lot of sliding doors that would not open before the door behind you had slid completely shut.

Once inside the interview room, I was always conscious that I only had limited time to conduct the interview. This meant that you had to interview in a very concise and focussed way. Normally, you were left on your own with an offender in a tiny room that was like a small booth. I could swear they had hidden listening devices in those rooms to enable them to listen in on discussions with the most serious of offenders.

Things were different when I had to interview a man accused of murder. The room was a bit larger and there was a Prison guard stood right behind me and one stood behind the offender throughout the interview. We were sat at a table and half way between the offender and myself was a small partition about the size of a table tennis net. Neither of us were permitted to pass any- thing or any part of our body over it. The murder involved a gangland execution of a drug dealer. You would imagine that the murderer would be a big, tough and scary man. However, he was in fact a small, weak, diminutive man who just sat there whinging and complaining all of the time. In talking about his life experiences, he described being bullied at school and also described being bullied during his short stay in the army because he said he had flat feet and could not march properly.

What is a Newton Hearing?
A Newton Hearing is where someone is pleading guilty to an offence but disputes one of the facts of the case. A hearing is held to determine whether the fact as outlined by the Prosecution is correct or not.

For example, I recall a case where a motorcycle courier admitted to pushing a traffic warden away from him with both his hands in a shoving action.

The traffic warden claimed that he had been knocked to the ground and that the courier had jumped up and down repeatedly on his legs causing extensive injury to the legs, necessitating fairly lengthy time off work.

The courier disputed the warden's version of events, stating he did not punch the warden to the ground or jump up and down on the warden's legs. A Newton Hearing was held at which the courier produced CCTV evidence showing that he shoved the traffic warden away with one big push with open hands, and then got on his motor bike and drove away. The CCTV footage clearly showed that he had not punched the warden to the ground and then jumped up and down on his legs, as claimed by the warden. The enterprising courier managed to obtain the security video footage from the office block, he had just delivered documents to.

Mr Summers took part in a new special scheme run by both by the Police and the Probation Service.

At about the time of this report, the Probation Service and the Police did set up a special project which involved supervising prolific offenders in an intensive way. The idea was that if you focussed your resources at the handful of prolific offenders offending in one area you could have a very positive impact in reducing the crime statistics for that area. The project was in fact very successful indeed.

One of the local Crown Court Judges headed up the

scheme. Orders were made out to the Judge under a special schedule and offenders were required to appear for regular progress reviews before the judge, which proved to be very motivational.

Supervision was intensive from both the Police and Probation. The offenders were asked to wear a 24-hour GPS tracking device which enabled the Police to monitor the offender's whereabouts at all times. From the offenders' point of view, this was very useful, if they were keen to stay out of trouble. Providing they were not involved; the GPS tracker would rule them out of being suspected of a crime when it occurred. Had they not been wearing the tag they would be suspected of committing the crime each time a crime occurred. In other words, those not wearing the tag used to get, annoyingly, very frequent visits from the police.

In return for agreeing to wear the tag, the offender would be offered every support in dealing with any problems or issues. Help would be given regards getting a job and finding accommodation if needed. Support would be given to address addictions if needed too.

Mr Summers came out of Prison on licence as part of the scheme. I was a member of the joint Police and Probation team and recall he benefited greatly from the intensive supervision and support on offer. He was allocated local authority accommodation. He got a job as a caretaker at one of the local churches and also helped run their food bank. He did well and eventually stopped offending altogether. However, it wasn't always as easy as it sounds, as I recall he did go through a period of experiencing mental health problems.

What was it like to work as a Probation Officer in a multi-agency team with the Police?

At the time it was a brand- new scheme and it felt really strange. For much of the week we were situated in a large room in the middle of a large Police Station. The cultures of both the Police and Probation Service were both very different. All over the walls of the large room we shared with the Police, were large A4 mug shots of the prolific offenders we were supervising. The number of tasks and workload of a Probation Officer seemed so much more than that of a Police Officer. I also got the impression that the Police were constantly trying to push us around and bully us. Things often used to come to a head over whether or not to breach someone and to have someone recalled to prison.

Recalling someone to prison requires quite a lot of checks and balances and a lot of work for a Probation Officer. A key component in recalling someone to prison is normally written evidence from the Police in the form of statements confirming that the person had been charged with an offence. However, the Police were constantly trying to get us to recall people in the first instance, without them charging the individual, or completing any statements or paperwork on them. It used to make me so cross.

However, I recall I really got on well with the Police Officer who administered the tagging scheme. In those days wearing a tag was voluntary and we were both good at persuading the offenders to wear one. In one of the towns, I worked in, there were relatively few black people living there. I was supervising a black person who was upset that every time that someone black committed an offence in the area, he would get a visit from the police. He took it personally and felt they had it in for him. I had to encourage him to keep a diary of his whereabouts, so that he could confirm that he was not in the vicinity of any crime being committed. I persuaded him to wear a tag and as it ruled him out of committing crimes. The visits from the police immediately stopped. Not only that, the police suddenly became much more friendly towards him and went out of their way to help him get a job at one of the local warehouses.

The Police in the team took the unusual view that you can keep arresting people and have them sent to Prison, but that the offenders have to be released at some point, and then this is the crucial time when efforts need to be made to stop them reoffending. This we did by close monitoring and control and providing lots of support.

Something that did concern me one day, was that one of the police officers made a pointed remark towards me and repeated something I had said in confidence to a third party on the telephone. It seemed to me that the only way they could have known this was by tapping either my phone, or the third party's phone.

One day, I accompanied a Police Officer in a panda car to go and visit an offender in prison together. The officer got fed up with the heavy traffic and put his siren on and all of the cars in front of us scattered out of our way. A little while later we stopped off in a service area and he flashed his police warrant card, which resulted in us getting two free cups of coffee.

Is there a common perception that the Courts are too lenient and that this is causing a rise in crime?

Several months ago, my son had his mobile phone stolen from him in London. We immediately reported the matter to two nearby police officers. They gave chase but did not manage to catch the offender. One of the police officers came back and apologised stating there was a lot of this sort of crime happening because we have a weak criminal justice system in this country. He said that those being arrested were being sent to Court and then dealt with much too leniently and that this was causing a crime wave. He might say that, but that is his opinion and where is the factual evidence to support this? Furthermore, one could express a lot of concerns about the current efficiency and effectiveness of the police. Police conviction rates have been falling and are currently at an all- time low.

Sentencing Mr Summers

What did Mr Summers look like?
Mr Summers looked like someone who had formerly been in the Army. He was tall, athletic, blue- eyed and had fair, light brown hair. However, he looked very tired and seemed quite thoughtful. I recall that he always considered me as being an experienced professional and that he was always friendly and respectful towards me. Nevertheless, he was scathing about some of his previous experiences of Probation.

> **What were the issues that Mr Summers was disputing for which he wanted a Newton Hearing?**
>
> **Why was Mr Summers upset with the Probation Service?**
>
> **What efforts has Mr Summers made towards stopping offending and towards leading a law-abiding life-style?**
>
> **In what way did Mr Summers help and co-operate with the Police?**
>
> **Why do you think Mr Summers chose to co-operate with the Police?**
>
> **What would you think of this Court report if you were Mr Summers?**

How high is the risk of Mr Summers reoffending?

Very low/ low / medium / high / very high?

What risk of harm does Mr Summers pose the public?

Very low/ low / medium / high / very high?

What events during Mr Summers' life do you think have contributed to him becoming an offender and what things could have helped him not offend?

What steps would you take to reduce Burglary Offences in the UK?

How would you sentence Mr Summers?

How would you go about motivating Mr Summers?

In what way do you think the Probation Service could treat Mr Summers differently?

Section 32

How People's Lives Can Change for the Better
Court Report 15

Outline of case:

This Report was prepared for Magistrates Court on a Barry Barley. The offence of theft took place two years ago and Mr Barley's life has changed considerably since.

Commentary on report 15.
I describe how I was assaulted once at the Probation Office on the last day of work before Christmas one year.

Instructions:
Imagine you are about to sentence Mr Barley

Carefully read through the following report. It is based upon a real person and real events that actually happened. All of the names of people and places have been changed as have some of the details of the defendant so as to protect their identity.

As you carefully read through the report, think about the facts of the case and what happened. Think about the actions of the defendant and the potential impact upon victims. Also carefully consider the defendant's behaviour and attitudes and their background.

Once you have read the report proceed onto the Commentary on Report 15 section and answer all of the questions before sentencing Mr Barley.

Please also give consideration as to what steps society could take towards reducing similar offences happening in future.

THE PROBATION SERVICE

This is a pre-sentence report as defined in Section 3(5) of the Criminal Justice Act 1991, it has been prepared in accordance with the National Standard for pre-sentence reports. It is a confidential document prepared specifically for this court hearing.

HARPERBURY MAGISTRATES COURT

Date of Hearing: 20.01. 1997

Full name: Barry Barley
Address: 26, Downtrodden Road Lower Ruttlesford

Date of Birth: 18.06.1973
age: 23 years

Offence
Obtain Property by deception 28/01/1994

petty sessions area: Ruttlesford

supervising court: Ruttlesford

Completion date: 2.01.1997

Report Produced by: Mr John Ebrington
official title: Probation Officer

Address:
Probation Office, Civic Centre Ruttlesford Home County. RU23 8P

1 Introduction

1.1. This report is based upon one office interview with Mr Barley when, as requested, he brought with him various documents which confirmed his background details. I have seen the Crown Prosecution papers and have discussed the contents with Mr Barley.

2 Offence Analysis

2.1. Over two days in January 1994, Mr Barley dishonestly obtained building materials and tools from a Builder's Merchants in Ruttlesford. This was a premeditated offence and he did this by falsely claiming to be an employee of a firm he used to work for. He filled out the company's purchase order forms in the name of another employee and then collected the items from the suppliers. The total value of the goods taken was £1,582. Mr Barley was eventually arrested for these offences in October 1996, when he promptly admitted his guilt in interview with the police.

2.2. Mr Barley says his motive for his offence was to obtain money from his previous employers who had not paid him for about a month despite his frequent requests for his weekly payment. As he had been contracted on a self-employed basis, he recalls that he re-submitted his invoices, but this was to no avail and he became frustrated with the situation. It is worth bearing in mind that he was 19 years old at the time of the offence. In discussing it with him, it is clear that he did not know how to go about obtaining legal redress, or even that free and impartial advice was available from someone such as the CAB. He was additionally living away from home at the time and had not been in contact with his parents for some time.

2.3. With the benefit of hindsight, he says he should have gone to see a solicitor but that at the time he did not know he could do this. Given nearly three years has elapsed since the offence, he no longer recalls the exact sum his former employers owed him. The firm state it was £985, but Mr Barley believes it may have been substantially more than this. He later sold the dishonestly obtained goods at a car boot sale and states he only got between £300 to £400 for them.

2.4. Mr Barley now acknowledges he should not have taken the law into his own hands. Furthermore, he realises his actions were devious and stupid and he now feels ashamed of committing the offence. Although he thought his former employers would have to pay for the goods, he explains that he did not realise that it was in fact the building suppliers who suffered the loss. He recognises they were an innocent party to the dispute and that thefts from such firms, if not controlled, could result in people losing their jobs. He says that he would like to take steps to compensate the victims.

3 Relevant information about the offender

3.1. Mr Barley's family originate from Lower Ruttlesford and he describes having experienced a normal and happy childhood growing up there. At secondary school he was a member of the swimming and athletics teams and played in goal for the football team. He says he found academic studies more difficult but gained 8 GCSE's at E and F grades.

3.2. After leaving school, Mr Barley was taken on an apprenticeship as a trainee electrician with one of his grandfather's friends who had a small electrical business. Whilst there he went to Howards-Gate College on day release and eventually gained a City and Guilds level one certificate in electrical instillations after passing a resit examination. Not long after qualifying Mr Barley gave in his notice to his employers, as he says he had concerns about the standards of their work and decided to look elsewhere. With the benefit of hindsight, Mr Barley says he regrets leaving his former employers, as he considers they "were very good to him".

3.3. Mr Barley also left home at about this time following arguments with his parents about his then girlfriend of whom they disapproved. He initially went to live with her, but the relationship was short-lived and he now reflects that his parents were right to have voiced concerns. However, Mr Barley did not return to live with his parents after the break up and he says that this was out of a false sense of pride. He took a job as a live in bar person and became good friends with a couple who were relief managers, before moving to live with them at their home in Havingstead. It was whilst he was living in Havingstead that he went worked for the firm of electrical contractors and the offence occurred.

3.4. Not long after the offence, Mr Barley went with a friend to work for a building firm in Germany doing labouring work and erecting scaffolds. His friend returned to England and Mr Barley stayed on in Germany and was taken on by a German firm. Mr Barley found it an enriching experience to be in another country, he began to learn to speak German and made friends with a German family. This family encouraged Mr Barley to renew contact with his parents at Christmas time and he returned to England in 1995, after having spent 18 months in Germany. He was 21 years old.

3.5. Mr Barley is now fully reconciled with his family and says he now gets on extremely well with his parents. He even, in a self-effacing way, pokes fun at himself, in stating that he takes after his grandfather, who he describes as being a stubborn individual. Since his return he successfully applied for work and trained as a bus driver with London Buses. He stayed with them for a year before moving on to become a coach driver for a firm in Surrey. Both jobs have involved a degree of responsibility in dealing with the public and handling cash. He says he feels settled in this job and that he enjoys taking pride in his work. He recently got engaged to his girlfriend at Christmas, who he has known for about 8 months and they are in the process of buying a house together. They have made an offer on a property and a building society has offered them a loan. Their repayments will be set at £364.00 per month.

4 Risk to the public of reoffending

4.1. Mr Barley was polite and co-operative in interview and does not present as being a violent individual. He has no record of previous offences and a period of almost three years has elapsed since the offence, during which time Mr Barley has stayed out of trouble, matured and settled down. He seems highly motivated towards ensuring that he does not re-offend and I believe that the risk of him doing so is low.

5 Conclusion

5.1. This is a serious offence given the value of the property dishonestly obtained. However, this offence occurred some time ago during a period when Mr Barley was living away from his family. He has since reconciled with them and striven to lead a law-abiding life. Should the Court take an exceptional view of the circumstances it could impose a Conditional Discharge which when coupled with a Compensation Order could serve as reminder of the Court's disapproval of Mr Barley's offence whilst retaining the court's sentencing powers should Mr Barley stray from his good intentions.

5.2. I have considered the option of a Probation Order with Mr Barley, but as there is no pattern of offending to address there would appear to be little purpose in imposing such an Order, apart from it merely being a reporting exercise.

5.3. In considering all the circumstances, I would propose the Court imposes a Community Service Order (also known as Unpaid Work) as it would suitably punish Mr Barley whilst enabling him to repay society constructively. At present Mr. Barley regularly works overtime on Saturdays for his firm and would have to give this up to do Unpaid Work, thereby representing a considerable punishment to him. I have explained the strict requirements of the Order to him and he indicates his willingness to comply.

John Ebrington
Probation Officer

YOU, THE SENTENCER - WHAT WOULD YOU CHOOSE?

Section 33

Assault at the Probation Office
Commentary on Report 15

Christmas Time
Mr Barley's report was prepared over Christmas time and reflecting upon it prompted me to recall what happened to me on the last day at work before Christmas one year. Some people get very stressed and wound up in the lead up to Christmas. It was about lunchtime when one of our regulars, who had mental health issues came into the office, in a very agitated state demanding to see someone. The Probation Officer on 'office duty' was summoned and quickly ushered him into an interview room. However, the shouting and banging on the table became so intense that someone at reception called the police. Concerned for my colleague, I went and hovered outside the interview room. Meanwhile, the police had arrived and were waiting outside of the building. Suddenly the man burst out of the interview room and almost walked into me whilst loudly demanding why was I standing there outside of the door. He became very aggressive and punched me twice in the face viciously. In doing so he sent my spectacles

flying across the room. Rather than react aggressively I immediately sat down into one of the waiting-room chairs and gestured for him to calm down. He did so and someone at reception told the police that he had now calmed down and that they could go. Somebody later said to me that there was no point involving the police as the man had mental health problems and every-one shortly went home for Christmas, except I had a very sore face through it being punched.

I didn't feel the situation was dealt with particularly well by management and the organisation. It didn't leave me feeling particularly valued as an employee either. Every-one seemed more intent upon going home for Christmas. I really feel that there should have been some sort of de-brief about what happened and for there to have been learning points for the organisation.

However, there was something that the organisation used to do well and that was called supervision. This was a monthly meeting with your line manager primarily to discuss the people you were supervising. It was really useful to be able to discuss cases that were of concern to you and your line manager was often able to give you really good advice. Your welfare and career development would also be discussed at the meeting.

Sentencing Mr Barley

What would you think of this Court report if you were Mr Barley?

How high is the risk of Mr Barley reoffending?

Very low/ low/ medium/ high/ very high?

What risk of harm does Mr Barley pose the public?

Very low/ low/ medium/ high / very high?

What do you think is the best way of reducing Mr Barley's offending?

How would you sentence Mr Barley?

What events during Mr Barley's life do you think have contributed to him becoming an Offender and what things could have helped him not offend?

What do you think the reasons for Mr Barley not being paid on time for his work?

Why do some companies prefer to employ their staff on a self-employed basis?

YOU, THE SENTENCER - WHAT WOULD YOU CHOOSE?

Section 34

A Man Obsessed About Cars

Court Report 16

A Different Court Report
Instead of the usual Court Report you have a Deferred Sentence Report to study. At the last hearing the Court deferred sentencing Mr Hope for a three- month period and he was given specific targets to achieve over the period. This report is letting the Court know how he got on over the period.

You are asked to read the short following report and decide upon whether you follow its recommendations.

Commentary on report 16
Robert Hope was a prolific offender from childhood who eventually came good.

Deferred Sentence Report

Introduction

1   Mr Hope appeared at Paddington Magistrates Court on the 02,02.97 when his sentence was deferred for three months. During the deferment he was to:

   a. Commit no further offences,

   b. Retain employment,

   c. Continue to co-operate with Probation.

Response to supervision

2   I can confirm that Mr Hope has satisfactorily completed the supervisory period of his licence which ended on the on the 04.04.97 and that he has remained in contact with me since that date on a voluntary basis. He has reported when instructed to do so and has made positive contributions to discussions. He has received much encouragement to take steps towards becoming a legal driver now that he is no longer disqualified. He tells me that he has been studying his highway code and that he intends to start taking driving lessons once he has saved up sufficient money.

3   Mr Hope seems to have made a positive effort to keep out of trouble and to stay away from his former

friends who feels may be involved in offending. He has continued to live at his sisters address in Potterham. I recently had a telephone conversation with his sister who said that she was pleased with his efforts and that he would be welcome to stay with her for as long as he wished.

Commit no further offences

4   To my knowledge Mr Hope has not committed any offences during this period.

Retain employment

5   Mr Hope has remained actively employed throughout the period of deferment. On the 18.02.97 he changed employment to work as a labourer for a local building firm. He is currently earning £200 per week before tax and deductions. From what he tells me he enjoys the job as his work involves very varied duties and that he is often trusted to work on his own un supervised. Mr Hope has never managed to obtain legitimate employment before this year. It is therefore encouraging that he appears to have settled in well into this job.

Mr Hope is assessed suitable for the imposition of a Community Service Order and or a Probation Order.

However, given the good progress Mr Hope has made over this period of deferment I respectfully suggest the

Court imposes a financial penalty for this offence.

John Ebrington
Probation Officer

Section 35

At Last, a Positive Outcome

Commentary on Report 16

(Deferred Sentence)

My knowledge of Peter Hope

Peter Hope was one of the first offenders I supervised and I recall I formed a positive relationship with him. I had to hang in there with him for several years before he eventually stopped offending altogether.

I recall that he grew up in a children's home and that he started offending as a young child, when he and other children stole sweets from a local sweet shop. As he grew up, his obsession became motor cars. This included stealing from them and taking vehicles "for joy rides". Basically, the term "joy ride" involves taking a vehicle without owners' consent. The sort of thing young Peter Hope would do, would be to break into a car and then take it for a drive before returning it to a street nearby.

Following being caught, he was sentenced to Young Offender Institution where he made friends, with more sophisticated offenders and learnt how to commit more crimes. He became quite institutionalised and the only friends he had were offenders.

Following his release from Young Offender Institution, he was recruited into a sophisticated criminal gang, who stole cars to order and then changed their identities, such as their colour and number plate etc, before putting them in a container and shipping them abroad. Peter Hope's only involvement was to steal the cars and then drive them to a garage where they would have their identities changed.

Another crime he did was that he went with a little van, parked up outside a row of millionaire's houses and then quietly broke into their garages and stole all of their bottles of champagne, bicycles and golf clubs.

Whilst he was serving a prison sentence for these crimes, he did a large poster sized drawing of my Citroen 2 CV car that was really excellent. I recall I said to him, "Why can't you do this sort of thing for a living, instead of crime."

He really did make a determined effort to stay out of trouble and not reoffend following his release from prison. He ended up working with one of his old ex-offender friends who similarly was determined to lead a law-abiding life-style. They set up a car valeting company together. They loved the work, were highly enthusiastic and were very successful indeed.

I lost touch with him when I moved to work in another area, but was really touched when about five years later, he managed to track me down and call me on the telephone, to let me know he was still doing really well and staying out of trouble. He had now moved to Scotland, was now married and had two children. He said that his only problem was that the locals were all making fun of his London accent. His work was otherwise going really well. Most importantly he was 'keeping his nose clean' and had not reoffended.

Sentencing Mr Hope

| **How would you sentence Peter Hope?**

Section 36

Upper-Class Man Commits an Offence

Court Report 17

Brief Outline of case

The case is at Crown Court and the defendant is Lord Hanbury aged 59 years old. His offence is Fraudulent Trading. Basically, Lord Hanbury, blew £9 million of his shareholders money without their permission upon failed South American investments fraudulently.

Commentary on report 17
Offenders can come from all walks of life including the upper classes and politicians. Shockingly high numbers of politicians fiddled their expenses several years ago. How austerity cuts and reforms made to Criminal Justice have ended in failure is discussed. Currently, from my perspective, the Probation Service appears to be in poor shape and to be struggling.

Instructions:

Imagine you are about to sentence Mr Lord Hanbury.

Carefully read through the following report. It is based upon a real person and real events that actually happened. All of the names of people and places have been changed as have some of the details of the defendant so as to protect their identity.

As you carefully read through the report, think about the facts of the case and what happened. Think about the actions of the defendant and the potential impact upon victims. Also carefully consider the defendant's behaviour and attitudes and their background.

Once you have read the report proceed onto the Commentary on Report 17 section and answer all of the questions before sentencing Lord Hanbury.

Please also give consideration as to what steps society could take towards reducing similar offences happening in future.

SECTION 36

THE PROBATION SERVICE

This is a pre-sentence report as defined in Section 3(5) of the Criminal Justice Act 1991, it has been prepared in accordance with the National Standard for pre-sentence reports. It is a confidential document prepared specifically for this court hearing.

CROWN COURT

Date of Hearing: 3.07. 1999

Full name: Lord Alfred Hanbury
Address: 58, Uptown Road   Middle Ruttlesford

age: 59 years

Offence: Fraud

petty sessions area: Ruttlesford

supervising court: Ruttlesford

Completion date: 02.07. 1999

Report Produced by: Mr John Ebrington
official title: Probation Officer

Address:
Probation Office, Civic Centre Ruttlesford   RU23 8P

1 Introduction

1.1. To prepare this report papers were obtained from the Crown Prosecution Service. One lengthy interview was held with the defendant. A discussion was held with the defendant's solicitors over the telephone. I had sight of a recent current account bank statement and a letter from Brompton Bank which confirms the defendant's monthly pension. I was shown a sworn statement of liabilities dated June 1999 and details of a loan with High Standard Bank. I have also had sight of a medical report prepared by Dr French of St Georges' Hospital

2 Offence analysis

2.1. The Court has indicated that it is taking a serious view of this offence and that it is considering all options in this case.

2.2. The circumstances surrounding the offence were that the defendant between January 1989 and March 1992 carried on the business of Parker Ltd with intent to defraud the creditors of the business by enabling the company to continue to support the South American ventures and to invest funds in Trump Worldwide Coal. He was acting to the potential prejudice of the Company's creditors. In view of the history of the South American ventures and the scale of the Company's liabilities, Lord Hanbury knew that there was a significant risk that the Company would not be able to meet its financial obligations should they fall due. It has been accepted that Lord Hanbury acted in the genuine expectation that the South American investments would be profitable and generate sufficient funds to repay all the loans.

2.3. Parker Ltd and its previously highly successful subsidiary Boothby Gin went bankrupt in 1992. The defendant told me that Boothby Gin was worth about £9 million at that time and that as a result of going bankrupt, the shareholders lost all their assets. There were 20 shareholders who were all members of the Hanbury family. Lord Hanbury said that apart from his aunt, they are all no longer on speaking terms with him. He believes that it was one of his brothers who alerted the Fraud Squad. According to Lord Hanbury, the Receivers sold Boothby Gin to Charles Snodgrass and as a result the majority of his 135 employees kept their jobs. Lord Hanbury told me a number of years previously he had set up a pension scheme for all the staff and that their pensions remained intact and unaffected by the bankruptcy. He said although the firm's suppliers initially lost money, they were apparently repaid about two thirds of what they were owed by the Receivers.

2.4. Lord Hanbury made it plain that his original intention was to make legitimate money for himself and the Shareholders by a genuine attempt to diversify and invest money in various South American companies such as Trump Worldwide Coal. However, Lord Hanbury said that he continued to invest money in the South American ventures, even though they were unsuccessful. He said that he took the view that they were under-capitalised and more likely to be successful with additional funds being invested in them. However, he admitted that he failed to keep his shareholders fully aware of the situation and avoided doing so. He told me that with the benefit of hindsight, he now feels that he should have pulled out in 1989, but foolishly continued in taking an unacceptable risk in Trump Worldwide Coal. He said that his motivation was that he was determined to become a successful businessman in his own right, but that he failed because he was too over optimistic and recognised that he had taken an unacceptable risk.

2.5. Lord Hanbury told me that he now recognises that his actions were highly irresponsible and reckless, particularly as it involved other people's money. He told me that Boothby Gin on its own had been a profitable enterprise that was making about £2 million profit per year. He conveyed that he felt ashamed of his actions stating, "dad would have been furious with me". Lord Hanbury told me that he had foolishly put everything on the line and now has substantial debts to South American companies, which are in his name. Trump Worldwide Coal was, he said, a legitimate business enterprise from which he did not draw a salary. He said that he had made a number of short-term loans that he is no longer able to pay back. He states that he began to feel sick with himself, when he realised that everything was going wrong and that he might not be able to pay people back. He recalls that he started to become very worried in 1987 and underwent a great deal of stress over the next five -year period.

2.6. In my assessment, the reasons for the offence appear to have been that Lord Hanbury took an unacceptable risk in gambling assets, that were not his, in the vain hope that he might become successful. It is relevant to note that there were proceedings against Lord Hanbury in 1993, brought by the Department of Trade and Industry, which resulted in him being disqualified for 9 years under the Company Disqualification Act 1986. The Fraud Squad arrested him for the current offence in August 1994. Matters have therefore been hanging over Lord Hanbury for an exceptionally lengthy period and he appears to have experienced stressful circumstances since the late 1980's.

3 Offender Assessment

3.1. The defendant was born in Aylesbury. He was the eldest of four boys and recalls having experienced a happy childhood. He attended Buckingham Prep School as a boarder before going on to Eton. He told me that he had a lovely' time there. Although not good at sports, he says he benefited from excellent teaching and gained three A levels with good grades, before going on to Oxford University in 1959. He said that his parents were keen for him to study Law, but chose to take Economics and Social Anthropology. He recalled that he had a good time at university and said that by gaining a 2.2, he had worked a lot less hard than students do nowadays.

3.2. In 1964, he left University and went on to complete a three- year Chartered Accountancy course. Then in 1967-8, he took a gap year and travelled with a friend to Mexico, Peru, Argentina, Paraguay and then for a short period in the USA. On his return he spent 18 months working for another Gin Company that belonged to friends of his family. He met his wife in 1969 and they married some six months later.

3.3. Lord Hanbury went into the family business, being the eldest of the brothers he was groomed for the role of running the Boothby Gin manufacturing company. It was felt that he had good skills for dealing with people and he became Managing Director in 1975.

3.4. The family subsidiary company Granville Ltd was wound up in 1979 following an unsuccessful decade of trading. Boothby Gin, meanwhile apparently prospered. Lord Hanbury began to delegate a number of activities within the work place and took up outside activities. In 1977, he became a lay magistrate at the local Magistrates Court and in 1979 he became a local Income Tax Commissioner. However, things changed in the mid 1980's. There was a change at the top in 1986, when Lord Hanbury became Company Chairman and Mr Smitt became Managing Director. Lord Hanbury took control of the family investment portfolio at around that time and began taking an interest in diversifying and investing money in other projects. Lord Hanbury resigned from the local bench in 1989. He said that he no longer had the time to be a Magistrate or a Tax Commissioner, particularly as these posts seemed to be attracting more administrative duties. He also stood down as president of Hartington's Gentleman's club in London.

3.5. Lord Hanbury advised me that his wife experienced a difficult period between 1969 and 1986 when she was diagnosed as being clinically depressed. The origins of the depression apparently lay in a disturbed childhood. Lord Hanbury told me that his wife hid her problem from their children and that she received treatment and group therapy over a lengthy period. Lord Hanbury said that he generally got on well with his wife, but as an aside, said that this was providing there was always adequate financial provision, for her and their children. She has nevertheless been supportive and stood by him through his difficulties. He told me that he felt that his wife had benefited greatly from the therapy and was now mentally a much tougher individual, who was able to help others. He said he felt his wife and his family were in some ways prepared for him to go to prison and would be able to cope. Nevertheless, his wife has been ill with back trouble since 1996, which she has found very debilitating. Her condition has required hospital treatment.

3.6. Lord Hanbury and his wife have seven children. Six of their children's ages range from 30 years down to 20 years respectively and the seventh child is 15 years old. Lord Hanbury told me that all the eldest children were sent to private boarding schools and consequently Lord Hanbury was faced with large bills for their school fees, particularly about 9 years ago when they were all at school. His youngest daughter is currently at a grant-assisted boarding school in Buckingham. He describes her as being very mature and level headed for her age. Lord Hanbury told me that he felt proud of his grown- up children as they had all gone through university and achieved well, in their own spheres of interest. He said he had been open with them about the Court proceedings against him and had encouraged the four eldest children to attend Court with him. He said that this was so that they could hear for themselves what was going on, as opposed to reading what he felt were distorted accounts in the media. He feels that a positive outcome of his troubles is that his children have grown up stronger and more able to fend for themselves.

3.7. Lord Hanbury and his family used to live in a 12 bed-roomed house in Chesham. This was sold in 1999 and I understand the proceeds went towards clearing Lord Hanbury's debts. Lord and Lady Hanbury now live in a three bed-roomed house in High Wycombe, which I understand is in fact owned by Lloyds of London. A statement of assets and liabilities confirms that Lord Hanbury has liabilities in excess of £1.5 million. Lord Hanbury showed me his current account, which confirmed that he currently has a modest income and expenditure. In accordance with agreements, he reached with them, he regularly pays £1,200 per month to his creditors. He has a pension plan, which pays him £24,000 nett per annum. In addition to this, he has a small part-time job in London working for a friend as an advisor. This pays him approximately £5,000 per year. Although this activity keeps him occupied, he actually makes little money from this after deducting his daily travel expenses.

3.8. The Court will have seen the medical report prepared by Dr French which confirms that Lord Hanbury is HIV positive and therefore at risk of AIDS. He told me that he contracted this virus through intravenous use of heroin in 1992. I was shocked by this disclosure of how he contracted the virus. I initially found his explanation hard to believe or comprehend. However, having discussed the issue at length with him, I understand that he felt under tremendous pressure in 1992 and he used this as a means to give him solace. He was introduced to the substance by someone he considered trustworthy, but obviously this was not the case. He states that he only used heroin over a short period of time and managed to wean himself off the substance.

4 Assessment of the Risk of Harm to the Public and Likelihood of Reoffending

4.1. It is my opinion that the risk of further offending is relatively low because Lord Hanbury has learned his lesson and no longer has the means to offend in the same manner. This is based upon my assessment of the defendant in interview, and examination of his social history.

4.2. Furthermore, there are no indications to suggest that Lord Hanbury is likely to pose a risk to the public through violent behaviour.

4.3. Lord Hanbury impresses as a man who feels little self-pity about his circumstances. He tends to understate things and hide his emotions. I imagine that this stems from his background and education. I gained the impression that he is taking full responsibility for what occurred when others could well have been involved. He seems not overly concerned as to what may happen to him today and appears remarkably composed about his predicament. In many ways he is looking forward to this matter being finally resolved as it has hung over him for several years. During this time, he has been unable to plan his future with any certainty and, furthermore, his life expectancy has been severely shortened, as mentioned in the medical report.

4.4. In my view, the defendant's capacity for change appears to be strong and his motivation appears to be high. In short, it is my view that he is highly unlikely to re-offend. I would recommend that Lord Hanbury, at his stage in life, changes direction and does something completely different. I think it would be healthy for him to make a break from his former business friends and find other things to do; i.e. undertaking an Open University course, doing charity work or working for one of his children. I discussed this with Lord Hanbury who seemed open to these ideas and very interested in forging a new life for himself.

5 Conclusion

5.1. In the light of the offence, the offender's circumstances and the risk assessment outlined above, I have looked at all the sentencing options. I have also taken into account the Court's initial indication of the seriousness of the offence. In the unlikely event of the Court considering a Community Sentence appropriate, I can confirm that Lord Hanbury is assessed suitable for both Probation supervision and Unpaid Community Service work

5.2. Given the large sums of money involved it seems likely that the Court will consider this case as being so serious as to merit a custodial sentence. Should this be the case, I would ask the Court to take account of the length of time that Lord Hanbury has been under pressure by having these matters hanging over him and his medical issues as outlined in Dr French's report in determining the length of his sentence.

John Ebrington
Probation Officer

Section 37

Concern Must Be Expressed About Our Politicians
Commentary on Court Report 17

Outcome of Case

Lord Hanbury as expected was sentenced to a custodial sentence. The first two months of his sentence, he spent in an old Victorian maximum- security prison, before being moved on to an Open Prison, populated by less dangerous offenders. The open prison was an old army camp where many of the inmates got involved in farming activities.

I had discussed with him the possibility of going to prison when I was preparing the Court Report and I recall him saying something along the lines of, "Oh, don't worry, it is just going to be like being sent back to boarding school for a bit. I will be fine." Even so, his time in the old Victorian prison must have been highly unpleasant.

I have also never heard the experience of being sent to

boarding school at Eton compared with being sent to prison before. However, I understand it does cost less to send someone to Eton than it does to prison.

Lord Hanbury did make himself useful in prison by helping those with poor literacy skills. He helped people write letters and helped to teach reading and writing.

When he was a magistrate, he regularly sentenced to people to terms of imprisonment and probably never thought any-thing of it. However, having experienced it himself I recall him telling me on leaving prison, that he thought it was awful and real waste of time and money. He joined the campaign for Prison reform and did a bit of charitable work for ex-prisoners, and I was pleased about that.

Offenders come from all walks of life, including a number of MP's, celebrities and people from the upper classes. From a Probation Officer's point of view, it is not uncommon for upper class type people to change their tune, from being a rather punitive, pro-prison type people, into keen advocates for Prison reform, once they had experienced prison for themselves. Lord Hanbury was no exception. For example, Jonathan Aitkin was a high- profile person who experienced imprisonment and then publicly supported Prison Reform.

Senior Politicians who broke the law.
It is worth remembering that it is not just the lower classes who break the law and get sent to prison for

their offences. A number of senior politicians have been found to have committed perjury and perverted the course of justice, in trying to protect their reputations and status. Perjury is an offence of deliberately telling an untruth under oath.

Jonathan Aitkin was a high- profile conservative MP in the 1990's, who became accused breaching ministerial rules, by accepting his stay at the Paris Ritz, be paid by an Arab businessman. There were also stories in the press, that he had precured sex workers for Saudi businessmen purchasing weapons from the UK. Jonathan Aitkin took legal action against those who had published these stories by accusing them of libel. However, Jonathan Aitkin was subsequently found to have attempted to pervert the course of justice and perjury in the hearing, for which he was sentenced to 18 months imprisonment in 1999.

Following his release from custody, he became a passionate advocate for Prison Reform. He also became active in the Church of England and later became a vicar.

In 2001, famous author, life peer, and former Deputy Conservative Party Chairman Jeffrey Archer was sentenced to four years imprisonment for perjury and perverting the course of justice. He was cast out of the Conservative Party for a period of five years, but has remained a life peer.

In 2013, former Cabinet Minister, Chris Huhne was

sentenced to eight months imprisonment for perverting the course of justice. The scandal ended his political career.

The Disgraceful Parliamentary Expenses Scandal

The parliamentary expenses scandal is one of the most disgraceful episodes in British History. In my opinion, the main lesson to be learnt from it, is that we the public need to select our politicians much more carefully and place them under much greater scrutiny once they are in office. It is simply not acceptable to have one rule for us and one for them.

This major political scandal emerged in 2009, concerning expenses claims made by members of both the House of Commons and the House of Lords. There were various sources for the expense claims, but they mostly gradually released in highly detailed instalments by the "Daily Telegraph". They revealed incredibly widespread misuse of expenses by our parliamentarians. The actual details of the claims left many of the public in the UK simply outraged and completely aghast. Some of the claims appeared to be for frankly ridiculous items. However, the majority of inflated expense claims seemed to be centred around second home allowances. For example, Chris Grayling was reported, in the press, as claiming for a second home, even though he lived only 17 miles away from Parliament.

As a result of the scandal there were many resignations, sackings, de-selections and retirement announcements.

The majority of those who had made over inflated expense claims were simply made to make a public apology and repay the money over paid. At the time, it was said that statistically you were more likely to come into contact with a criminal walking around parliament than you were walking around in the general public.

A total of four MPs and two peers were prosecuted and sentenced to terms of imprisonment for falsifying their expenses. MP David Chaytor fraudulently claimed more than £20,000 in expenses and was sentenced to 18 months imprisonment for his offence. MP Jim Devine was jailed for 16 months for falsely claiming more than £8,000. MP Elliot Morley was sentenced to a year's imprisonment for fraudulently claiming £30,000. Lord Hanningfield and Lord Taylor were both sentenced to custodial sentences for their fraudulent expense claims.

The whole expenses scandal severely tarnished the already poor reputation of politicians.

Even a number of UK celebrities have criminal convictions.

Quite a number of celebrities have gained criminal convictions. Steven Fry when he was young, was sentenced to three months imprisonment for fraudulently using someone else's credit card. Celebrity TV chef Gino D'A Campo, was sentenced to two years imprisonment for a Burglary offence he committed when he was young. Cheryl Cole was convicted of assault.

One Direction singer Louis Tomlinson was convicted for assaulting a paparazzi, as was Russell Brand. Steven Gerrard gained a conviction for assaulting someone in a night club. Boy George gained a conviction for assault and false imprisonment. Most worrying of all were the offences of Rolf Harris, Jimmy Saville and Gary Glitter who all committed a series of sexual-offences against minors and vulnerable individuals.

Lord Brocket
In 1996, Lord Brocket was sentenced to seven years imprisonment for an insurance fraud and obtaining money by deception. Apparently desperate for money, following making a huge loss at Brocket Hall, Lord Brocket buried some of his classic car collection in the grounds and then fraudulently claimed they had been stolen. Eton-educated Brocket, once a lieutenant in the Army, had an awful time in prison. He was punched, kicked, slashed with a razor and repeatedly threatened. When he was eventually released from Prison, he zoomed past the assembled press, waiting to interview him, on a motorbike with a helmet on his head hiding his face.

Politicians and Public servants
Many public servants will tell you, that their quality of working life is very much influenced by the politicians in charge of them. Often, this was down to the individual minister in charge. Things could change tremendously from one Minister to another even if they were from the same party.

When I started working for the Probation Service, I recall we had a really good minister in charge of us. He genuinely seemed to believe in us and trust us to do a good job, as a worthwhile alternative to imprisonment. He used to consult with us, which was much appreciated by us.

Although a member of the same political party, we then had a completely different type of minister sometime later. Stories began to appear in the press that he was considering replacing the existing Probation Officers with Army Officers. His mantra was to be tough on crime and kept stating, "Prison Works."

They also brought in a new system which seemed rather tough on us. If one of the offenders you were supervising committed a serious further offence, it would result in the work you did with that offender being investigated by a senior manager. The files would be seized overnight and then gone through with a fine toothcomb. You then had to attend an interview with a senior manager, who would hold you to account, on whether you had done the job properly and in a timely manner. I recall attending one of these interviews and remember it feeling, it was like attending a disciplinary interview. It also felt a bit rich, as we were all regularly working more hours, than they were paying us for, just to meet the demands of the job. If something went wrong, it felt like the individual Probation Officer was going to be hung out to dry, rather than the organisation as a whole.

Sometime later there was a new Government and another change of direction. We were now to be asked to undertake complex risk assessments on each offender. This involved completing a lengthy form on the computer and these were quality checked by our line managers. The Government set targets on the completion of these forms and Probation funding was dependent upon us meeting these targets. Suddenly the emphasis of our work seemed to change from face-to-face rehabilitation work to doing these risk assessments. At times, it really felt like we were becoming a form filling factory.

When Chris Grayling became our Minister the Probation Service was eventually, torn apart and transformed into a dysfunctional organisation by his actions. He split the Probation Service into two. One half was privatised and the other half remained within the public sector. Staff who had been working together for many years were forced to choose which half they wanted to be in. It was chaotic. Imagine splitting a secondary school in half and making half of it, public sector and privatising the other half. It didn't work. Most damaging of all, was that really skilled and experienced staff simply left or were made redundant.

Grayling's reforms took place in 2014 and within five years they were assessed as being a very costly failure. The private companies on the whole failed to provide sufficiently good enough services. Reoffending rates went up, as well as recalls back to prison for beaches of prison licences, went up significantly. In 2019, the audit commission announced that the Probation service should be renationalised and that the process would cost the tax payer an additional £467 million.

Sadly, many good and experienced Probation Officers have left the Probation Service over the last ten years and continue to do so. Caseloads have risen to unacceptably high levels and staff appear to be leaving because they are finding the job too much to cope with. Currently, the Probation Service appears to be in poor shape. In my opinion as a consequence of this, there is currently a high risk of mistakes occasionally occurring in the management of serious offenders. I only hope individual staff do not get blamed for these mistakes, when clearly the responsibilities lie elsewhere.

Grayling also made drastic cuts and reforms to the legal aid system which came into effect in 2013. The result of this has, in my opinion, been disastrous. People's access to legal advice for family, housing, employment and criminal matters has radically reduced. Many solicitors now no longer do any legal aid work and numerous legal advice centres have closed down. The few outlets that still offer limited access to legal aid, now tend to be staffed by less experienced professionals. Many people now end up having to represent themselves in Court. This has contributed to more pressure being placed upon the courts and to court processes slowing down. I also fear numbers of miscarriages of justice may go up too.

When it comes to funding cuts, the Criminal Justice agencies such as the Prisons, Courts and the Probation Service are probably the easiest to hit. The cuts all went under the radar and you get the feeling the public, could not careless about these agencies either.

I feel passionately, that we as a society, should be much more concerned about finding ways of stopping our future citizens becoming offenders in the first place and more concerned about rehabilitating those that do. Simply adopting a more caring approach towards each other in society, and in the world, would be a good starting point in my view.

In the next Chapter, I shall be encouraging you to start adopting this very approach by posing you numerous questions to think about. I hope you enjoy this section and find it stimulating.

Sentencing Lord Handbury

What did Lord Hanbury look like?
He looked like a stiff, well-dressed upper class English man. He seemed very reserved and quite humbled by coming into contact with the Criminal Justice system.

> What would you think of this Court report if you were Lord Hanbury?
>
> What is different about Lord Hanbury's upbringing

and background as compared with the other offenders in this book?

Why do you think Lord Hanbury offended?

What health issues did Lord Hanbury have and how did these come about?

What impact has the offence had upon Lord Hanbury and his family?

How high is the risk of Lord Hanbury reoffending?

Very low / low / medium / high / very high?

What risk of harm does Lord Hanbury pose the public?

Very low / low / medium / high / very high?

How would you sentence Lord Hanbury?

If Lord Hanbury poses a low risk of harm and low risk of reoffending what is the point of sentencing him to a custodial sentence?

What events during Lord Hanbury's life do you think have contributed to him becoming an Offender and what things could have helped him not offend?

Do you think Fraud is on the increase in the UK, and if so, why do you think it is?

What steps could society take to reduce Fraud offences?

Section 38

What Would You Choose?

1   What would you do if you were driving along and you hit a dog?

    The law states that you must stop and report the incident to the police.

    Did you know this?

    Yes / No

    Did you know that you would be breaking the law if you failed to notify the police?

    Do you think people should be taught this sort of thing at school?

    Should you hit a dog when you are driving, it is best to pull over as soon as it is safe to do so. If the animal has a collar on it with the owner's name and address and or phone number on it, you can notify the details to the police. You could also contact the owners to let them know what has happened.

However, if you hit a cat you don't have to stop and advise the police of the incident. If you find an address on the cat's collar you should, as a matter of courtesy, advise the owners about what has happened.

2   What would you do if you found a lost dog?

Would you?

a) Take it to the local Police station

b) Take it home with you

c) Contact the owners if their details are on the collar

d) Contact the local dog warden

You should try to identify the dog's owner by looking for an address on its collar. If the dog has no address or collar, you should contact the local authority dog warden.

Years ago, I did take a young dog, that was obviously a family pet, that had got lost from its family, to the local police station and they then contacted the local authority dog warden for me. I think these days the expectation would be that you contact the dog warden direct yourself.

Did you know, that if you cannot identify the owner yourself, and you decide to take the dog home temporarily, then by law, you must inform your local authority dog warden so that the authorities can take up responsibility for finding their owner?

3   **What would you do if you found £100,000 in cash in a bag in a local park?**

Would you?

a) Keep the money for yourself

b) Hand it to the Police

c) Give the money to Charity

KEEP THE MONEY FOR YOURSELF:

It is tempting to keep the money for yourself. Just think of all of the useful things you could do with the money. As we grow up many of us learn the saying "finders' keepers, losers' weepers". Even if you don't keep all of the money for yourself you could give some of it to charity.

But before taking the money, have a think about how did the money get there. Could it be money left there as payment for a ransom and police officers are lurking in the bushes waiting for the person who is coming to collect the ransom?

Could it be money that has been dropped by a bank robber?

Perhaps the money could be something to do with an illegal drug deal. Would you really like anything to do with drug dealers? No thank you.

What would you do if all of the notes have the same serial number on it? Would that mean that the money is counterfeit and would you take it home for yourself under such circumstances?

You never know, the money may even have been planted there by a TV company to film how people react to finding the money.

HAND THE MONEY TO THE POLICE:

This is the right thing to do. I know that we are not taught this at school but finding a large sum of money and then keeping it for yourself is a criminal offence. It is called "Theft by Finding", and you can be prosecuted for such an offence.

Some young 12- year- old boys, recently found a large sum of money at a local railway station. They split the money evenly between the four of them and went home with the money. One of the mothers, who was very concerned about this, spoke to all of the other mothers and rounded up the boys and organised them to hand it all of the money at the local police station.

As no-one came to claim the money as lost property from the police, the money was handed back to the boys six months later.

4 What would you do if you found that your bank had accidently transferred £20,000 into your bank account by mistake?

Would you?

a) Not say anything to the bank and spend it all straight away

b) Notify the bank of their mistake and make the money available to them in full

KEEP AND SPEND THE MONEY

It would be a criminal offence to do this. The bank would ask you for the money back and if you were unable to repay it, they may very likely take steps to prosecute you. I recall during my early days in the Probation Service in the late 1980's seeing six Barclays Bank customers prosecuted for this. They had all had large sums of money accidentally paid into their account, said nothing about it to the bank and then spent all of the money.

In Chapter 17 is the case of 62- year- old grandmother Melody Larkins, who was unable to repay the money she had been accidentally over paid by the Post Office. She was prosecuted for theft.

NOTIFY THE BANK OF THEIR MISTAKE AND MAKE THE MONEY AVAILABLE

This is the correct thing to do. Basically, if you find anything of value you should make every attempt to reunite it with its owner.

I recently lost my wallet in a local street and recovered it almost straight away. The person who found my wallet found my phone number written inside and called me. I went round their house and was impressed that all of the cash and cards that I had left in the wallet were still there. It was also apparent that the people who had found the wallet were poor people and that was really touching. I gave them an award for their kindness and honesty by later dropping off a thank you card together with a store gift card for them.

5. **What would you do if you find a burglar in your house in your kitchen and he has a knife in his hand?**

Would you?

a) Pick up a knife

b) Pick up a broom

c) Run into your bathroom, lock the door and call the police

RUN INTO THE BATHROOM

My advice would be to run into the bathroom, lock the door and call the police. But if you are cut off from the bathroom and feel the need to defend yourself the best weapon to pick up would in my opinion, be the broom. I think you would have more chance of fending off the burglar with the broom than the knife.

PICK UP THE KNIFE

The problem in picking up the knife, is that you could be at risk of harming the burglar quite seriously, even perhaps killing the burglar with the knife.

You are permitted to use appropriate force in order to defend yourself but you should not really exceed this.

Sentencers will carefully consider each case on its

merits and will consider what are the aggravating and mitigating features of the case. Defending your home from an armed burglar is more likely to be given considerably more mitigation than another case involving someone defending themselves with a knife in a public place, where the carrying of knives is not permitted.

I recall one case where two men got into a fight outside of a night club over a girlfriend. One man got punched in the jaw, which was broken, then fell to the floor and then his ribs were fractured by being kicked in the ribs. The other man was unscathed and was prosecuted for the offence of GBH. (Causing Grievous Bodily Harm).

The man who was prosecuted felt it was unfair, as he said that it was not him that had started the fight. He maintained that he was attacked by the other man as he left the night club and caused the injuries in defending himself.

In this case, it would appear that the view was taken that he had not used appropriate restraint in defending himself and had kicked the man on the ground. He had broken the law by causing GBH, but in mitigation had been provoked, as the other man had attacked him in the first instance.

In 1999, a farmer shot dead a 16-year-old burglar in the back. He lay in waiting for the burglar before the shooting and his actions were viewed as being excessive and premeditated. He was originally convicted of murder but this was later reduced to manslaughter. His custodial sentence was subsequently reduced following a diagnosis of mental health problems.

In the UK, it is illegal to carry self-defence weapons in public. The maximum sentence for possessing a weapon in the UK is six years in prison, whilst possessing firearms is ten years.

Whilst, the police are permitted to use pepper sprays the public are not allowed to have them at all.

6 In the UK is it alright to?

a) If somebody shouts rude abuse to you in public is okay for you to shout rude abuse back?

b) If an unarmed burglar enters your home, is it alright to shoot them dead?

c) If someone hits you over the head with a bottle in a pub, is it okay to do the same to them?

d) If someone cuts you up on the road, is it okay to sound your horn aggressively and then cut them up yourself?

e) If your employer under pays you, is it okay for you to steal items from them to the equivalent amount?

f) If someone offers you something that has been stolen, is it okay to accept it?

g) Is it okay to queue jump at a tube station?

h) If everybody else is speeding along the road, is it okay for you to do the same?

i) If you are going to a fancy dress party, is it okay to be dressed as a Police Officer, walking through a town centre dressed in the costume?

The answer in my opinion should be no to all questions in section 6, as if you answer yes, to any, it could involve you breaking the law.

Section 39

Difficult Dilemmas

In this section are some difficult dilemmas that are best usefully debated amongst a group of people if possible. By doing this, I am hoping to encourage people to adopt a more considerate approach towards each other in society.

1 **You are at a railway station. An old lady comes up to you and asks you for the money for her train fare home.**

   What do you do?

   a) Give her the cash

   b) Offer no money, but to phone home for her

   c) Tell her to seek assistance from the British Transport Police

This dilemma is based upon a true story of a little

elderly lady who was supplementing her income by doing this at Kings Cross Station. She was not really travelling and was conning people out of their money. Whilst trying to be kind and considerate it is best to avoid becoming completely gullible.

2   Your son is 21 years old and still believes in Father Christmas. Should you do anything about it?

3   What would you do if your friend asked you if she looked nice in a dress and she looked really ridiculous and awful?

   a) Tell her she looked awful and ridiculous

   b) Tell her she looked absolutely fabulous

   c) Tell her that some people might like it but that it is not one of your favourites and that you prefer her in one of her others.

4   You hear your neighbours having a violent argument. What do you do?

   a) Do nothing

   b) Call the police

I would recommend calling the police. Whilst they might not need to take action, it is important that they take note and log the incident. It is important that every instance is noted by the police. The victim may need support. Also, it might not be appropriate for someone to be bailed to an address where such instances are occurring.

5. **My daughter has the offer of marriage of two men:**

   a) A romantic poet who she is extremely fond of, but is very poor and lives in a bedsit.

   b) A very stable man, extremely rich and 20 years her senior, but she does not love him.

   Which man should she choose?

6. **What do you do if you buy something in a shop and the assistant gives you too much change?**

   a) Do nothing

   b) Thank your lucky stars

   c) Point it out and give the over- paid amount back

7 **You are in a supermarket when another shopper appears to be following you around and to be staring at you continuously. What do you do?**

a) Tell them to leave you alone and to go away

b) Quickly move away continuously

c) Ask them, do I know you?

It later transpires that you were at Primary school together!

8 **Please advise my friend Sarah. She has a ten -year-old son who wants to stay over- night for a sleep over with his school pal George. His pal George is a good lad and his Mum is lovely. However, Sarah is really worried about the Mum's new boyfriend who seems strange and Sarah has a really bad gut feeling about him.**

What do you advise Sarah to do? Should she allow her son to go, or are there any alternative actions she could take?

In my opinion gut feelings are very important.

9 **Your friend steals some cakes from a shop and passes you one. What do you do?**

10 You put your bag through the security machine at the airport. You then notice that the attendant has fallen asleep and is not checking the bags. What do you do?

   a) Do nothing

   b) Gently wake up the attendant and ask them if they are okay

   c) Bring the situation to the attention of a supervisor

This situation actually happened to a friend of mine who brought the sleeping security guard to the attention of a supervisor and as a result everybody's bag in the departure lounge was checked again.

11 You see your neighbour watering their garden with a hosepipe during a drought when there is a hosepipe ban in force. What do you do?

   a) Dial 999 and call the police

   b) Advise your neighbour about the ban in a friendly manner

   c) Get your hosepipe out and squirt your neighbour with water.

12 You are on an evening out in a pub with your friends. One of your friends is so drunk that they can no longer stand up without falling over. The pub landlord seems annoyed about the situation.

   What do you do?

   a) All leave the pub and leave the drunk behind for the Landlord to deal with.

   b) Make sure the drunk gets home safely, by taking them home straightaway.

   c) Let the drunk sleep it off a bit and then help them make themselves sick in the toilet.

   Apparently, in law, it is the Landlord's responsibility to ensure that no-one is drunk at the pub. If you get drunk, the law states the Landlord can refuse to serve you, ask you to leave, or even make arrangements for you to be arrested by the police for being drunk and disorderly in a pub.

13 You are superstitious about the number 13. You have just viewed a lovely house for sale and would like to make an offer to buy it. Unfortunately, the house is Number 13, in the street. What do you do?

   a) Don't make an offer to buy the house as you could not possibly live at a house numbered 13.

b) Just make an offer and don't worry about it.

c) Make an offer to buy the house and when you move in, change its number from 13 to 12a.

14 My manager is making my life difficult at work. She really dislikes me. No matter how hard I try, my work is never good enough for her. She is also belittling me behind my back to my colleagues. It is difficult for me to complain as she is the one, I am supposed to go to if I have any issues. What should I do?

15 What would you do if you saw someone stealing razor blades in a supermarket?

   a) Challenge the person and tell them to put them back

   b) Pretend you didn't see them

   c) Quietly report them to a member of staff

16 Your friend is really struggling to pay his mortgage, gas and electricity bills. What do you advise him to do?

17 You are in a restaurant and your friends want to split the bill equally.   They have had lots of alcohol and deserts. You only had a small starter salad and tap water. What would you do?

18 Please advise Laura who has a friend called Sue. Her friend Sue keeps choosing the wrong men to have relationships with and then keeps drinking too much. Sue keeps calling up Laura in the middle of the night and telling Laura all of her problems. Sue is always crying, very drunk and talking at length when she calls Laura. Laura does care for Sue. What do you advise Laura to do?

19 You are at a football match and you see a fan commit criminal damage by ripping out one of the seats. What do you do?

20 Your friend asks you to look over their application form, they are about to submit for a job and you notice that they have falsely claimed that they have a qualification that they don't actually have. What do you do?

Could your friend be breaking the law? In short, yes. I recall writing a report about someone falsely claiming they had a Diploma in Social Work, when they didn't. The person got offered a job on the strength of this and later got charged with committing an offence of 'Pecuniary Advantage'.

21 You feel your colleague is being bullied by one of the managers where you work. What do you do about it?

22 You feel one of your friends may have been in the process of being unfairly dismissed from their job. What do you do about it?

23 Your 14- year- old daughter shared an intimate photo of herself with her boyfriend who has now forwarded it on to his friends at the local boy's school. His friends have also shared it with their friends. One of the other parents has brought it to your attention. You are also aware that it is against the law to share indecent photos of an under 18- year- old in the UK. What do you do?

24 Your friend has trouble sleeping at night. What advice do you give them?

25 Your friend is really struggling with their university studies. What do you advise them to do?

26 Your friend is feeling very depressed. What can you do to help them? What can you do advise them to do?

27 You are parking your car in a car park and you accidentally dent and scrape another car whilst you are parking. You have caused quite serious damage, but no-one has seen you do it. What do you do?

28 Suicides amongst young people in your local community have been increasing. What steps could be taken towards reducing these from happening in future?

29 You are very fond of your car and enjoy having conversations with it. However, as you are driving along your car has recently been telling you increasingly serious things for you to do. This concerns you. What do you think you could do about it?

30 Your teenage daughter is feeling increasingly extremely anxious about her exams and choosing a career path to aim for. When you were her age, the options only seemed to be for a woman to do hairdressing, or find herself a rich man. However,

you did manage to go to university later in life, when you were in your mid- thirties. Based upon your own life experiences, what advice do you give your daughter?

31 You are a defence solicitor and your client tells you about crimes that they have committed that the police are unaware of. Should you tell the police?

32 You are a nurse in a hospital. A patient's family is visiting and you are aware the patient is probably going to die within the next 24 hours. Should you tell the family?

33 Phoebe is 14 years old and thinks she might be pregnant. What advice and support can you give her?

34 It is 2am and you are at a party. All of your friends have gone home and you don't know any-body there. Someone offers you a lift home and you really like them, but you feel uncertain that they may have been drinking and taking drugs. You don't have a mobile phone with you. What do you do? Do you accept the offer of a lift?

35 Your friend is worried that their partner may have dementia. What advice and support would you offer them?

36 You have £5,000 which you must use for charitable purposes. What would you do with it?

37 You have two children aged 9 and 7. You live next to a deprived area that has a high crime rate. What steps can you take to help ensure your children don't get involved in criminality as they grow up?

38 Your 19 -year- old son is about to be released from Young Offender Institution having been sentenced to 6 months imprisonment. What sort of issues and problems do you think your son will face following his release? What can you do to help ensure that he does not re-offend?

39   As you drive around your local area you notice that there is an awful lot of litter everywhere. What do you think could be done about it?

40 You are abroad in a country, where there appears to be few people who are willing or able to speak in English and you are having a lot of problems communicating with them as you don't speak their language. How do you feel about it and what do you do?

41 You are in England and someone approaches you speaking very loudly, at you in a foreign language, that sounds like it could be German and you do not understand any-thing they are saying. How do you feel about it and what do you do?

42 You are in your local neighbourhood and someone who is deaf approaches you. They appear to be in a distressed state, but you do not understand what they are trying to communicate with you. How do you feel about it and what do you do?

43 You are advised that your twelve- year- old child has stopped attending school. What do you do?

44 Somebody expresses views that you consider to be racist to you. What do you do?

45 Your 14 -year- old son seems to be disengaged, of low self-esteem and to be under achieving at school. What do you do?

46 Why are girls increasingly out performing boys academically at school in the UK? What could be done to improve the boys' performance?

47 Britain is facing an obesity crisis amongst our children. What do you think can be done about it?

48 You are a headteacher of a secondary school. You are concerned that the boys at your school appear to be growing up lacking in empathy and sensitivity. What can you do about it?

49 Exclusions from the local secondary schools in your area have gone up by 70% this year. Why do you think this may have happened and what could be done to radically reduce the numbers of exclusions?

50 If you had a magic wand and could change our Houses of Parliament and the way we are governed, what would you do?

51 Numbers of people voting in UK local and General Elections appear to be reducing year upon year. Why do you think this may be happening and what do you think could be done to reverse the trend?

52 Please come up with at least six different ways that we could reduce crime levels in the UK over the next 20 years? Once you have selected all of your

measures that you would take to reduce crime, please identify the one single, measure you think would have the greatest impact upon reducing crime levels.

53 Quite a significant number of former army personnel, appear to be getting arrested for committing offences, following leaving the army. Why do you think this is and what do you think could be done about it?

54 High numbers of offenders reoffend upon being released from Prison. Why do you think this is and what do you think could be done about it?

55 You are a 14 -year- old girl and your best friend, who is also 14 years old tells you she thinks she may be pregnant and she asks you to keep it secret. What do you do?

56 You are a 14- year- old girl and one of the boys at your school has sent you an explicit photo of his genitals. What do you do about it?

57 You are a 14- year- old boy and you find your best friend, who is also a 14- year -old boy, drunk and

unconscious in the school grounds having drunk a lot of vodka. What do you do?

58 You own a local company that has about 50 members of staff. The current economic climate is such that you are unable to give them a pay rise. However, unfortunately you currently have very high staff turnover. Many staff are leaving and this is proving costly. You are now having to spend a lot of time and money recruiting new staff and training them. What steps can you take to reduce staff turnover without being able to give every-one a pay rise?

59 Some men in your company appear to be totally dominating the monthly staff team meetings and the women present in the meetings, never seem to take an opportunity to speak. What do you propose to do about this?

60 The Post Office Horizon scandal was a huge miscarriage of justice and has cost this nation millions of pounds. What do you think could be done to ensure such a thing never happens again?

61 You have a close friend who tells you that they are considering undergoing a gender re-assignment.

What questions would you ask and what advice would you give your friend?

62 Knife crime has been rising steadily in your area over the past five years. Why do you think this might be? What steps do you propose to stop this rise and to reduce knife crime?

63 Domestic violence has been rising steadily in your area over the past five years. Why do you think this might be? What steps do you propose to stop this rise and to reduce domestic violence?

64 There are a high number of Assault Police Officer offences in your area. Why do you think this is and what steps do you propose to reduce this?

65 In studying the Assault Police cases in your area, you note that there are two officers who have significantly more assaults committed against them than any other officers. Why do you think this is and what could be done to reduce the assaults upon them?

66 There appear to be high levels of Hate crime in the UK. Why do you think this is and what do you think

could be done to reduce it?

67 There have been a number of instances of valuable rings going missing from the fingers of elderly women with dementia whilst they are in the care of a care home and the NHS. The rings appear to be going missing following an ambulance being called and the elderly person being taken to Hospital. It is unclear where the rings are disappearing, whether it is at the Care Home, in the ambulance, or at the Hospital. Why do you think this has been happening?   What measures do you think need to be taken to stop these rings going missing?

68 What could be done to reduce the high number of suicides in the UK ? What could also be done to help those closely affected by them?

69 A six-year-old child suddenly completely stops talking at school. This condition is known as selective mutism. What do you think might have caused this to occur and   what kind of support could be given to the child?

70 What do you feel are the main lessons to be learnt from the Covid Pandemic, both for you personally, but also wider society. What changes do you

feel need to be implemented as a result of these lessons learnt?

71 England has not won the Football World Cup, since 1966. Why do you think this is ? What things do you think England need to do now, in order to improve their chances of winning the World Cup?

72 The UK is facing a mounting obesity crisis. Why do you think this is? What do you propose doing to address this issue?

73 Over 50 years ago, all of the postal services and a significant proportion of freight used to go by train. Today, this has dwindled to almost zero, as it is now nearly all transported by lorry on the roads instead. Why do you think this has happened? Do you consider this has had a negative impact upon the environment? What in your opinion could be done to reverse this trend?

74 The UK used to have one of the highest under teen-age pregnancy rates in the developed world. However, the Nuffield Trust reports that between 2007 and 2021, the under 18 conception rates, in England and Wales decreased by 68%. Is this a good thing and if so, why? How has this reduction been achieved and how can this reduction be

maintained?

75 Some County-Councils in England are reporting large increases of Ketamine misuse in their local areas in recent years. Increasing numbers of young people are reported to be misusing the drug. The drug seems easily available, illegally, and people do not appear aware of the health problems associated with misusing this drug. In particular, it can cause very serious long-term bladder problems. What actions do you suggest be taken to tackle this Ketamine misuse problem?

76 Does the UK have a 'sick note' culture? Politicians have been stating that it does. What do they mean? If the UK does have a 'sick note' culture what can be done to reverse it?

77 How satisfied are you with Politicians and the way we are governed in this country? If you are dissatisfied, what changes do you think could be made to improve the situation?

78 How can the world go about improving the situation in the Middle-East? What steps do you think could be taken towards achieving long-term peace?

79 According to the 'Their World' Charity, it was estimated in 2018, that there were about 65.6 million people around the world who had been forced out of their homes. Out of these were nearly 22.5 million refugees. Throughout the world there were 10 million stateless people. They were without nationality and basic rights such as education, healthcare and freedom of movement. The situation has not improved since 2018. What steps do you feel the world could take to improve the refugee situation in the world?

80 It is so difficult for young people to get on the housing ladder these days. Why is this ? What do you feel could be done to improve the situation?

81 Theft from shop offences are apparently at record high levels in the UK. Why do you think this is? What could be done to resolve the situation and reduce the number of these crimes being committed?

82 There has been a significant rise in Fraud offences being committed in the UK. Why do you think this is? What could be done to tackle this offending?

Thank you for reading this book

I would be very grateful if you could leave a review on Amazon about this book.

I do hope you have enjoyed reading this book and the interactive and participative aspects of it.

You are more than welcome to contact the author John Ebrington, with any comments and suggestions about this book by email: ebringtonjohn@gmail.com

- or on the Facebook page:
You, the Sentencer what would you choose?

https://fb.me/e/xYxiEyV5m

John Ebrington also has a YouTube Channel, where further interesting anecdotal stories and discussions about Criminal Justice and Probation can be found.

Do please check it out. To do this simply put John Ebrington in the YouTube search section.

Best wishes

John Ebrington
(John Ebrington is a pseudonym)

Printed in Great Britain
by Amazon